SCREEN WARS

SCREEN
WARS

Win the Battle for Attention
with Convergent TV

MICHAEL BEACH

**SCREEN WARS
MEDIA**

SCREEN WARS

Win the Battle for Attention with Convergent TV

First Edition

ISBN   979-8-9902298-0-8   *Hardcover*

979-8-9902298-1-5   *Paperback*

979-8-9902298-2-2   *Ebook*

For my beautiful bride, Brooke,
and our four amazing children,
Grace, Charlie, Graham, and Julia

CONTENTS

PART 2. HOW TV ADVERTISING WILL WORK IN THE FUTURE

PART 3. WINNING THE BATTLE FOR ATTENTION WITH CONVERGENT TV

ONE

INTRODUCTION

THE FIRST TV AD

Have you ever seen the very **first** TV commercial?

It aired on July **1, 1941**, on the television station WNBT (now known as WNBC). The ad for Bulova watches was **10** seconds long and cost only **$9** (**$181** in **2022** dollars): **$5** for station charges and **$4** for airtime.

It was nothing fancy. The black-and-white TV ad showed a round, analog clock face centered on top of a map of the US. On the clock, the words "Bulova" and "Watch Time" appeared prominently. A confident male voice announced, "America runs on Bulova time."

That was it. Do a YouTube search, and you'll see the ad for yourself.

That **10**-second spot was a far cry from today's visually rich commercials, but the flashy, clever ads we're now accustomed to all trace their origins back to this simple one. Only a few **thousand** people viewed the commercial, since not many households had television sets.

TV, the new medium, had arrived on the scene. When that brief Bulova commercial aired, radio advertising was huge, and radio ads continued to dominate the scene for years. Surely many at the time didn't see it yet, but ultimately, TV spots would catch up to and even surpass radio advertising. By **2010**, TV advertising in the US had grown to nearly **$59B**, accounting for more than **1** out of every **3** dollars spent on advertising (**$157B**).

Sound familiar?

THE GROUND IS SHAKING

A revolutionary shift similar to the transition from radio to TV is now happening with television advertising. You already know how far linear TV advertising has come since **1941**. That **first** ad aired over **80** years ago, but think about advertising in the past decade or so. The pace of change has accelerated even further. Things aren't as they once were.

The advertising world is constantly changing. Because of the continual shifts, you probably feel like the ground beneath your feet is shaking, and you want to find stability. What worked **80** years ago won't work now. But what about what worked even **5** years ago? Will that still hold up? While some factors, such as the **3** hours a day Americans spend in front of TV screens, have stayed

> ▶ **QUICK DEFINITION**
>
> **Linear TV**: The traditional television system in which a viewer watches a scheduled TV program when it's broadcasted and on its original channel.

fairly constant for the past **25** years or so, Americans now collectively spend **450M+** hours per day watching streaming services that did not even exist **10 to 15** years ago.

With this new technology, our attention has changed and adapted. Around **2012**, people's viewing habits began shifting dramatically. They were still spending plenty of time watching TV, but they also started spending an increasing amount of time in front of other screens and watching videos online. The audience was fragmented, and with streaming on the horizon, it was likely only to become even more fragmented. That split raised new questions: How could we effectively reach these people when they could be watching almost anything, at any time, on a wide variety of devices? What was the right mix of advertising to reach them?

In today's world, attention is more divided than ever, giving advertisers a big headache. Viewers now watch video on a wide variety of platforms and screens, making it more challenging than ever for advertisers to select the right mix of broadcast, cable, and streaming TV advertising to ensure they get their message in front of the right audience. As advertising dollars once migrated from radio to television, they're now flowing into streaming.

As an advertiser, you need eyeballs and attention, so you need to know what your target audience is watching. Is it television screens? Digital screens? Streaming? Should you split your budget equally among all available formats and hope for the best?

Thankfully, there's a better way than just guessing. To gain viewers' attention and support across a growing number of platforms, advertisers must formulate plans and design campaigns that successfully navigate an increasingly fragmented media landscape. Failing

▶ **QUICK DEFINITIONS**

Broadcast TV: Television that is delivered over the air via terrestrial antenna systems

Cable TV: Television that is delivered locally via coaxial cable or fiber-optic transmission

Streaming TV: An online service that allows subscribers to watch TV shows and movies over the internet (Netflix, Hulu, etc.)

Connected TV (CTV): Any television connected directly to the internet for video streaming

Note: I use "streaming TV" and "CTV" interchangeably throughout this book.

to do so might mean the difference between winning and losing your clients. But how do you devise successful advertising campaigns and effectively split them across multiple media?

Understanding and capitalizing on the paradigm shift is the focus of this book.

WINNING THE BATTLE FOR ATTENTION WITH CONVERGENT TV

You can't find your path forward if you don't have a map. This book will zoom out to give you the bigger picture of what you need to know in this changing environment. By the end, you'll understand how the advertising landscape has shifted, where it is headed, and how you should approach it in the future.

The content is broken into 3 parts to not only allow you to grasp the importance of the past but also ultimately help you feel confident in your way forward. Part **I** gives you important context via a history of the medium of TV, since consumers and technology have dramatically altered the landscape of video advertising; discusses how we watch TV; and addresses how the way we watch TV is changing. Part **II** delves into how TV advertising will work in the future, and Part **III** brings it home with an explanation of the battle for attention. Most importantly, I'll address how you can win that battle through convergent TV and be victorious in the ongoing Screen Wars.

At the end of each chapter, I tie the research and information together with a "Why This Matters" section, where I reiterate the most important facts and recap why that information is important for you to know.

How do I know what matters to you? Because I've been in your shoes and felt the frustration of not knowing how to split advertising budgets. I've specialized in this area for over a decade, and I've even built an entire company focused on optimizing every buy. Instead of guessing, we know how to use data and analytics to develop an optimal cross-screen strategy.

My background in developing this approach started in politics, where the outcome of advertising was just like the battle for attention today: zero-sum. In politics, it's life or death. Starting in **2004**, my focus in campaigns was on using analytics and data to figure out the right people to talk to and what to say to them to convince them to vote for our candidates. By the time I was **27**, I was overseeing a budget of **$120M** and had **dozens** of people working for me. In those early years, we spent most of our budget on direct-mail advertising, telemarketing, and going door-to-door. The internet was emerging, but we only spent

$50K (**0.04%**) on digital ads. These were mainly banner ads and some search-engine ads—nothing like what's available today.

I quickly realized that in future elections, the internet and social media would be used not only to release news and solicit donations but also to persuade and mobilize voters. Data and analytics would be used to target voters online. We would use the agility and speed of the digital world to test ads, measure the response, and make instant adjustments. Whereas in the past, we'd use analytics to know which neighborhoods to send door knockers to, now we'd use analytics to know which websites and social media to target to find precisely the type of voter likely to respond to our messages and support our candidates.

The opportunity to accurately and convincingly target voters with digital advertising prompted me to cofound Targeted Victory in **2009** with my business partner, Zac Moffatt. Our company pioneered using digital marketing to target voters, and we quickly attracted **hundreds** of clients, **$250M** in revenue, and more than **130** employees.

We became the conduit connecting campaigns nationwide to digital companies in Silicon Valley, with their rich behavioral data about voters. The tech companies did not understand political campaigns or how to reach the **thousands** of campaigns launched across all **50** states. And the individual campaigns scattered across the nation had no idea how to navigate a labyrinthine online world. We sat in the middle and created the infrastructure that connected **thousands** of political campaigns with Silicon Valley.

By the **fourth** year of Targeted Victory's existence (circa **2011–2012**), digital advertising had grown so much that it became difficult for advertisers to determine the right budget allocation between digital video and TV advertising. In **2012**, we highlighted the profound implications of voters not watching TV—and therefore not seeing the political ads—with a white paper titled "Off The Grid." In it, we broke down the data much like I'll break it down in this book: with what you need to know, why you need to know it, and how it affects you, the advertiser. We also concluded that the shift in media consumption behavior should be viewed not as an obstacle but rather as an opportunity. I still make that assertion in this book, but you need to know how to capitalize on the chance.

▶ **QUICK DEFINITION**

Behavioral Data/Targeting: The targeting of a group of people or an audience, based on their affinity or likelihood to perform a particular behavior (purchase a sedan, apply for an insurance quote, etc.); behavioral targeting is more accurate than untargeted advertising but less accurate than **first-party** targeting methods.

Every dollar you spend on an ad that misses the mark is a dollar wasted. The bottom line is if your target customer never sees your ad, nothing else you do matters. It won't matter how good your ad is or how often you run it. My goal is to help you maximize your advertising budgets and those of your clients. To do that, we must start by looking at how we got to where we are today.

Let's turn on the screens and press rewind to look at some history.

▶ **QUICK DEFINITION**

Digital Video Advertising: Any ad delivered on a digital device, including mobile phones, tablets, desktop computers, and connected televisions (CTV).

Note: Sometimes I will include streaming TV/ CTV with digital video, and at other times, it will be separated out.

TWO

12% OF OUR LIFE = WATCHING TV

OUR REAL PASTIME

The phrase "national pastime" may make you think of baseball, but Americans' *real* favorite leisure activity is watching TV.

Three hundred million Americans spend about **3** hours a day in front of a television (linear TV only).[1] This staggering amount accounts for **12%** of the average American's entire life. That's not counting their time watching videos on their smartphone or tablet. The average home has at least **2** TVs,[2,3] and more than **80%** of Americans watch TV on a given day.[4]

This behavior is nothing new. We've been watching a lot of TV for years. The amount of time we spend watching has only grown about **11%** (**+28** minutes) in the last **25** years, so we've been transfixed by our sets for a generation.[5,6] Cable, VCRs, DVRs, and streaming have only given us different ways to use the massive amounts of time we have always committed to TV.

We spend more time watching TV than on all other leisure activities combined. More than **half** of our nonsleeping and nonworking hours are spent watching TV. When everyone's time is counted, Americans spend about **1.5B** hours a day watching.[7] And that is before we even get to streaming TV, which currently takes up another **1.5** hours per day and is growing fast.

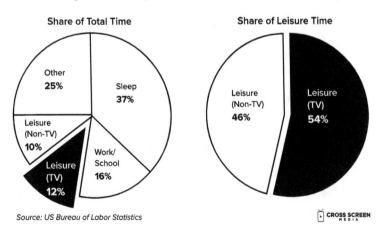

The Average American Spends 12% of Their Entire Life Watching TV

Share of Total Time

Share of Leisure Time

Other **25%**
Sleep **37%**
Leisure (Non-TV) **10%**
Work/School **16%**
Leisure (TV) **12%**

Leisure (Non-TV) **46%**
Leisure (TV) **54%**

Source: US Bureau of Labor Statistics

CROSS SCREEN MEDIA

WHAT IS "TV," ANYWAY?

You may find all this confusing, so let's simplify things. For the purposes of this book, we'll define "TV" as the shows you watch on the big screens in your home. It might be broadcast, cable, streaming, or a combination. TV-like content consumed on small screens—smartphones and tablets, for example—will not be included in our definition of TV.

TV IS CHANGING RAPIDLY

Recall from the introduction that today, we collectively spend **450M+** hours per day watching streaming services that did not even exist **10 to 15** years ago. While **50** years ago, Americans settled down in front of their TV trays to watch *The Wonderful World of Disney* every Sunday at 7 p.m. sharp, on-demand now lets us watch whatever we want, whenever we want. We can watch on a big flat-screen or on our phones. We can watch in the living room, in the car, or on the bus.

Streaming, unlike linear TV, has unlimited shelf space. There is no grid. The old TV model created scarcity, since each network only had **six** 30-minute slots to fill each night in primetime. This scarcity led to generic shows that could appeal to the widest audience. Streaming has blown that model apart. Whereas there were once only **3** channels (ABC, CBS, and NBC) filled with generic content, soon each person will have their own individualized channel with content recommended based on their interests.

> **KEY BATTLE IN THE SCREEN WARS**
>
> Offering this customized "channel" is a focus of giants such as Google, Netflix, Roku, Amazon, and Comcast.
>
> . . . .

All of these shifts are flipping the economics of the TV world on their head. Today, **61%**[8] of Americans still subscribe to a pay-TV bundle (cable, satellite, etc.), but nearly **90%** now also have subscriptions to Netflix, Amazon Prime, or Disney+.[9]

Once somebody starts streaming TV, they are likely to cancel their pay-TV service. Only **38%** of US homes have both pay-TV and streaming.[10] In **2022**, **5M** people cut the cord, bringing the total number of households without a pay-TV bundle to **48M** (**39%**).[11]

> **QUICK DEFINITION**
>
> **Pay-TV**: A bundle of TV networks, such as a cable TV package, purchased as a subscription
>
> *Note: I sometimes use pay-TV and cable interchangeably.*
>
> . . . .

Cord-cutting is starting to impact overall consumption. In **2022**, people spent more time watching TV through streaming than with pay-TV bundles.[12]

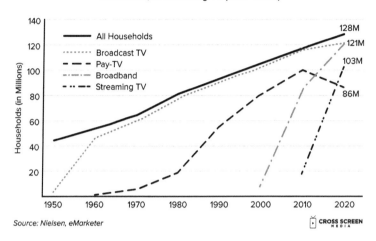

US Households with Broadcast, Pay-,
Broadband, or Streaming TV (1950–2020)

Source: Nielsen, eMarketer

▶ **WHY THIS MATTERS**

Americans will spend **12%** of their entire life
watching TV. For advertisers, there is no
better medium to reach potential customers.

THREE

WHAT IS CONVERGENT TV, AND WHY DOES IT MATTER?

WHAT IS CONVERGENT TV?

Convergent TV combines linear TV (broadcast, cable, and satellite) with streaming TV/CTV, programming delivered via the internet. This definition expands the idea of TV consumption to include all forms of video consumption, from the *60 Minutes* program we watch on Sundays at **8** p.m. on cable or broadcast to the shows on Netflix, HBO Max, and other streaming services we watch whenever we want.

Convergent TV is a unified ecosystem that aligns with consumers' modern, cross-screen viewing habits. With the appropriate technology, marketers can create unified, convergent TV campaigns that combine the broad reach of linear TV with the latest targeting, planning, and measurement opportunities of streaming TV. This approach combines the best of both worlds and enables advertising to reach target audiences precisely and efficiently at the hyperlocal level, regardless of how that audience consumes video.

This convergent TV landscape makes media buying dramatically different from the traditional linear TV approach of buying ads on **3** channels to run in different time slots. The convergent landscape is far more complex, but the opportunity it presents to reach wider and more discrete audiences is tremendous.

▶ **QUICK DEFINITIONS**

Convergent TV: Linear TV + Streaming TV

Measurement: Finding out the actual reach, frequency, and outcomes of an advertising campaign; cross-screen measurement is increasingly critical as advertisers place ads across linear TV, CTV, and digital video

WHY DOES CONVERGENT TV MATTER?

Eventually, all TV will be streamed. It may take some time to complete that transition (**2030** might be a good estimate), but the trend is well underway. We have never witnessed a technology get adopted this fast. Nearly **90%** of US TV households subscribe to a streaming service, up from **60%** in **2015**.[13]

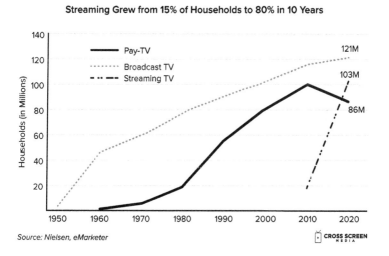

Streaming Grew from 15% of Households to 80% in 10 Years

Source: Nielsen, eMarketer

Despite trend lines traveling in opposite directions, we'll continue to live in a world of both linear and streaming TV for at least another decade. Baby boomers remain largely devoted to cable, and linear TV remains the most popular medium for live events. A great example of linear TV's hold on live events is the Super Bowl. In **2022**, **112M** viewers watched the Super Bowl, and only **11M** viewers (**10%** of the total) streamed the event.[14] Live events such as sports will be the last content to fully convert to streaming.

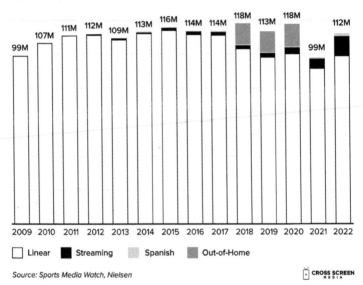

Super Bowl 2022: Streaming +96%, Total Viewers +15%

Linear ☐ Streaming ■ Spanish ▨ Out-of-Home ▨

Source: Sports Media Watch, Nielsen   CROSS SCREEN MEDIA

With that said, streaming use has exploded in America. According to a **2022** Nielsen report, streaming owns a **38%** share of total TV viewing in the US (↑ **38%** YoY)—while cable consumption was at **31%** (↓ **17%** YoY) and broadcast share was **25%**.

At the same time that our consumption is shifting to new networks (Netflix, YouTube, etc.), we are seeing an explosion in the amount of content produced. In **2010**, there were **216** scripted shows. By **2015**, there were **422**. In **2022**, there were nearly **600**.[15]

For years, a small number of TV networks determined what you could watch and when it would air. Now, consumers have more control over which services and programming they will pay for as well as when and where they'll watch.

For you, this means advertisers now have more choices, too. Linear TV advertising is leveling off. **Sixty-seven percent** of national TV advertising is dominated by a **few hundred** brands, and they often have to wait months to learn if their ad was effective.[16] Meanwhile, streaming ads are exploding as more advertisers see the value of targeted ads and rich, immediate data about the effectiveness of those ads.

With the explosion of programming and viewers now controlling when, what, and where they watch, the challenge for advertisers is finding their audience in this thick and tangled jungle of shows and viewing options.

▶ **WHY THIS MATTERS**

Linear TV and streaming will continue to "converge" into the **2030s**. As consumer habits change, advertisers will continue to adapt their TV advertising.

FOUR

WHY THIS BOOK?

SCREEN WARS VS. STREAMING WARS

Why did I call this book *Screen Wars* as opposed to *Streaming Wars*? That is a great question. I view the shift from linear to streaming TV as a single battle in the overall Screen Wars. As we enter the **2030s,** viewers' attention will continue to fragment across screens, many of which are brand new (virtual reality, digital out-of-home, etc.).

KEY QUESTIONS THAT I WILL ANSWER

As I've already noted, the TV landscape is changing rapidly. Neither linear nor streaming TV reaches everyone, and I don't expect that to change for several years. We are in a transition that will eventually lead to all TV being streamed, but advertisers will include linear and streaming TV in their media plans into the next decade. While this shift is complicating advertisers' plans, it is wreaking havoc on the business models of everyone from TV networks and pay-TV systems (cable TV, etc.) to Hollywood studios.

These dynamics are key to understanding how the Screen Wars will play out. Understanding the Screen Wars is the key to understanding how your customers will consume content in the future. As Wayne Gretzky famously stated, "I skate to where the puck is going to be, not where it has been."[17]

This book is meant to help you skate to where the puck is going to be. To do that, I am going to cover the following 3 fundamental topics:

1. How we watch TV
2. How TV advertising will work in the future
3. Winning the battle for attention with convergent TV

In Part I, I will walk through the history of TV content/consumption and the dramatic changes since Netflix launched streaming 15 years ago.

> **WHY THIS MATTERS**

TV dominates consumer media consumption (3 hours per day), but more platforms compete for that time than ever before.

PART

1

HOW WE
WATCH TV

FIVE

THE MAGIC TUBE

FIRST TVs EMERGE

It's hard to say who invented the **first** TV. Many individuals contributed. Charles Jenkins sent a still image over radio waves in **1922**, and John Baird sent the **first** live transmission in **1925**.[18] The following year, he demonstrated his device, called the televisor, in a department store.

The biggest breakthrough came from Philo Farnsworth, who filed a patent for the **first** completely electronic TV in **1927**. Other inventors set to work improving the transmission and image resolution, and by **1936**, RCA was able to provide the equipment that the German company Telefunken needed to broadcast the Berlin Summer Olympics.

During the **1939** World's Fair, RCA unveiled a publicly accessible TV. Franklin Delano Roosevelt became the **first** president televised, and televisions went on sale the next day as RCA and NBC began regular broadcasts. In **1941**, the FCC recognized television as a new medium, established technical standards for TV sets, and began approving commercial TV stations. Before World War **II**, there were fewer than **5K** total TV sets in operation, but that was about to change in a big way.

TV ADOPTION EXPLODES

In **1946**, about **8K** homes in the US had a television set. Within **5** years, there were **4M**.[19] During the **1950s**, the percentage of American homes with TVs grew from **9%** to

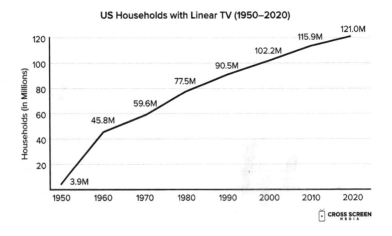

US Households with Linear TV (1950–2020)

nearly **90%**, and by **1980, 96%** of the country's homes had a TV. Adoption of black-and-white TVs in US homes significantly outpaced that of all other inventions up to that point.

TOP SHOW BY DECADE

TV history is filled with memorable shows. From *Texaco Star Theater*, the top show in **1950–1951**, to *The Big Bang Theory*, the top show in **2017–2018**, programs have worked their way into our cultural experience.[20] Some have a

Top-Rated Non-Sports Show (1950–2010)

Year	Show	Rating	% Change
1950	TEXACO STAR THEATER	61.6	
1960	GUNSMOKE	37.3	−39%
1970	MARCUS WELBY, M.D.	29.6	−21%
1980	DALLAS	34.5	+17%
1990	Cheers	21.3	−38%
2000	SURVIVOR	17.4	−18%
2010	the BIG BANG THEORY	14.5	−17%

Source: Wikipedia

CROSS SCREEN MEDIA

lengthy history all their own. *60 Minutes* has been on for **43** seasons, and *Monday Night Football* has been on for **32**. Some shows, such as *M*A*S*H* and *Friends*, were on for only **10** years but survived for generations longer through syndicated reruns and streaming.

To get a sense of how fragmented audiences have become, let's go back to **1983** and look at what happened when the final episode of the long-running hit *M*A*S*H* aired on CBS. More than **106M** viewers (**60%** of all US households) tuned in.[21] No other scripted TV show has ever come close to that number. The next closest show was Cheers, whose final episode in **1993** attracted **80M** viewers (**44%** of all US households).[22,23] When *M*A*S*H*

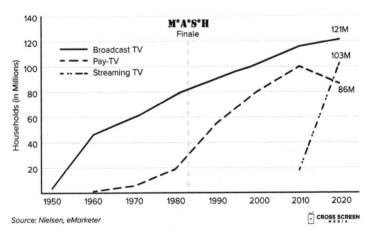

In 1983, There Were Only 3 Broadcast Networks and Less than 25% of Households Had Pay-TV

M*A*S*H Finale

Broadcast TV
Pay-TV
Streaming TV

121M
103M
86M

Source: Nielsen, eMarketer

CROSS SCREEN MEDIA

signed off, less than 25% of US homes had cable TV, and there were only 3 broadcast networks (ABC, CBS, and NBC). Fox hadn't launched yet.

Fast forward to 2019, when HBO aired the final episode of *Game of Thrones*. *GOT* ran from 2011 to 2019 and was the most-watched show on the network, ranked higher than *Euphoria* (number 2) and *The Sopranos* (number 3).[24] Its finale, "The Iron Throne," was highly anticipated. But its viewership was 19M—less than a fifth of *M*A*S*H*'s audience. While *M*A*S*H* was up against 2 other shows in most households in 1983, *Game of Thrones* was up against thousands of viewing options.

▶ **WHY THIS MATTERS**

Comparing ratings/ viewership for programs today to past decades is apples and oranges. Although people still have the same amount of attention (5 hours a day for convergent TV), it is now fragmented across thousands of choices.

SIX

100 CHANNELS AND NOTHING IS ON

THE CABLE COWBOYS AND THE BIRTH OF CABLE TV

One of the nation's **first** community antenna television (CATV) systems was created in **1950** in Lansford, Pennsylvania, whose access to Philadelphia stations was cut off by the Allegheny Mountains.[25] An appliance salesman erected a master antenna and hooked his subscribers to it with coaxial cable. Subscriptions cost **$3** per month after a staggering (at the time) **$125** installation fee.[26] Something similar happened in Astoria, Oregon, where a radio station owner erected a huge antenna to collect TV signals from Seattle. By **1952**, there were **70** similar systems around the country, and over the next **10** years, the number grew to **700**.[27]

Broadcast TV was free, but cable was expensive. It had to be Running a coaxial cable from house to house cost a lot, and for its **first 24** years, cable was primarily used to connect remote areas where the reception was poor. Expensive infrastructure costs convinced many that cable's growth was limited.

The early cable pioneers—"cable cowboys" like Bob Magness and John Malone of TCI—relied heavily on loans to build the cable infrastructure. At **one** point, TCI owed **15** times its revenue, a huge debt load.[28] But as the number of subscribers increased, revenue began to catch up to and then exceed debt payments.

From **1970** to **1990**, the percentage of US homes with cable grew from **8%** to **59%**.[29] Satellite distribution ushered in CNN, MTV, and a slew of "narrowcast" stations that provided niche content to discrete audiences, including the Christian Broadcasting Network, ESPN, Nickelodeon, the Home Shopping Network, AMC, A&E, BET, Discovery, and The Disney Channel. By **2010**, there were more than **100M** homes with cable service, which amounted to approximately **85%** of all households.[30]

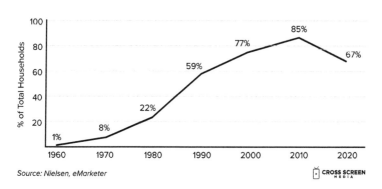

Pay-TV Penetration Peaked at 85% of All Households

Source: Nielsen, eMarketer

As the popularity of cable grew, companies serving as cable and satellite TV providers formed, giving rise to giants like Comcast, Cox, Dish, and DirecTV.

NICHE CONTENT THRIVES

Before cable became widely available, practically everyone sat down at **8** o'clock at night to watch a popular show like *Leave It to Beaver* on **1** of the **3** major networks. Advertisers had a built-in audience, and big networks controlled what we watched and when we could watch it.

But with cable, viewers had options. Cable networks splintered audiences toward different types of niche content, with some people preferring **24**-hour news or **24**-hour sports channels. Audiences' options increased even more when Home Box Office launched in **1972** and began transmitting its programming nationwide. HBO was a new source of revenue for cable companies, and people loved it. With HBO, subscribers gained access to shows that the major networks of the time wouldn't carry, such as *The Larry Sanders Show*, *Tales from the Crypt*, and *Sex and the City.* HBO's breakthrough use of satellite technology also opened the door for other premium television networks to emerge, including STARZ and Showtime.

From **1995** to **2015**, the number of cable channels exploded from **40** to **201**.[31,32] The problem, which would become clear later, was that the average pay-TV household watched less than **8%** of the channels they were paying for.

Number of TV Channels Has Grown 7X Faster than Channels Watched

Source: Nielsen   CROSS SCREEN MEDIA

In **1996**, the Telecommunications Act removed regulatory barriers and allowed cable companies to expand their services to provide telephone or telecom services, giving rise to megamergers like AT&T and Comcast. By the early **2000s, millions** of American homes were using cable for internet access and telephone services.[33] Many foresaw an "information superhighway" that was never fully realized by the cable TV companies, but the broadband pipes they were laying would become a necessary piece of infrastructure for streaming TV's rise.

CORD-CUTTING BEGINS

As previously mentioned, cable subscriptions grew for decades. They peaked in **2010** with over **100M** subscribers (**85%** of all US households). However, over the next **12** years, cable would lose **24%** of that audience and fall to **76M** subscribers (less than **67%** of all US households).[34]

While many blame the increasing popularity of streaming for cable's decline, the industry's staggering price increases played a major role. Remember earlier when I talked about how average pay-TV households only watched **8%** of the networks they were paying for? Well, another way to look at this would be they never watched **92%** of the networks they were paying for. Essentially, the pay-TV business was so lucrative that there was enough money to pay monthly affiliate fees to **200+** networks. Most skipped over these channels on their guide but were paying for them just the same.

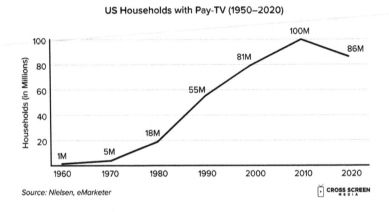

US Households with Pay-TV (1950–2020)

Source: Nielsen, eMarketer

CROSS SCREEN MEDIA

▶ **QUICK DEFINITIONS**

Affiliate Fees/Revenue (aka "Carriage Fees"): The fees paid to networks (ESPN, etc.) by pay-TV providers (Comcast, etc.) for the right to carry a channel.

Compound Annual Growth Rate (CAGR): Average annual growth rate over a period of time (years, etc.)

In **1995**, a basic cable package cost a little over **$20** per month.[35] By **2015**, it was nearly **$70**. That is a compound annual growth rate (CAGR) of **6%**, vs. **2%** for inflation during that time period. That means the price of cable TV grew at roughly **3X** the inflation rate over a 20-year period.

ESPN is ground **zero** for rising pay-TV bills. Since **2010**, it has grown affiliate revenue (subscriptions) from **$5.2B** to **$7.5B** (↑**42%**) while losing **20M** subscribers.[36]

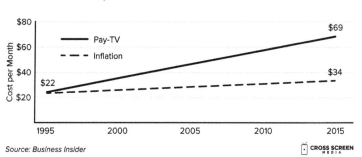

The Price of Pay-TV Grew at 3X the Rate of Inflation over 20 Years

Source: Business Insider

How has ESPN accomplished this marvel, you ask? It has been able to raise prices faster than subscriber losses. Since **2010**, it has increased the monthly fee from **$4.39** to **$7.62** (↑**74%**), or roughly **3X** faster than subscribers have canceled.

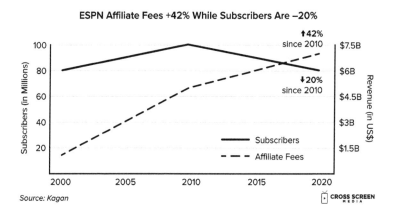

ESPN Affiliate Fees +42% While Subscribers Are −20%

Source: Kagan

The Price of ESPN Rose 74% While Subscribers Dropped 20%

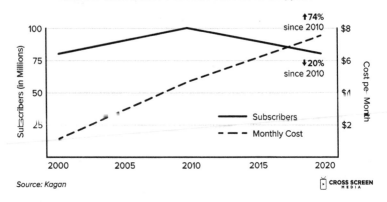

Source: Kagan

CROSS SCREEN MEDIA

▶ WHY THIS MATTERS

Each of the **76M** pay-TV households is paying **$90** per year for ESPN, but on any given night, only 3% (**1.9M**)[37] are watching the channel.

US Households with Pay-TV or Broadband (1960–2020)

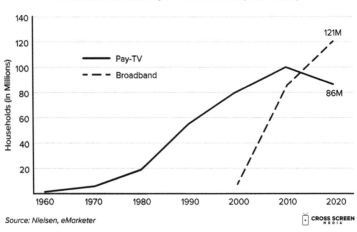

Source: Nielsen, eMarketer

CROSS SCREEN MEDIA

Over the past decade, **24M** households have canceled their pay-TV subscription. On the surface this appears to be devastating news for cable companies, until you consider the most important piece of infrastructure needed for streaming: broadband. It is hard to believe, but in **2000,** there were only **7M** households (**7%**) with broadband. By **2010,** that number had grown **1,095%** to **85M** (**72%** of all households).

▶ **WHY THIS MATTERS**

Broadband is the future for pay-TV companies such as Comcast and Charter. In the long run, they could generate more profit from broadband than pay-TV in its prime.

SEVEN

THE ALBANIAN ARMY TAKES OVER THE WORLD

IT ALL STARTED WITH DVDS

Just as cable disrupted traditional broadcast television, streaming services began challenging cable's dominance in **2007**, when Netflix first allowed customers to stream movies and shows on demand. Netflix launched in **1997** as a mail-order DVD-rental business. By **2020**, it was **1** of the biggest TV and movie studios in the world, with more US subscribers than all of cable TV.[38]

Despite its remarkable growth and financial success, Netflix struggled at times. In **2000**, for example, it nearly went out of business when the dot-com bubble burst.[39]

Netflix approached market-leading Blockbuster Video about investing and was laughed out of the boardroom. Jeff Bezos of Amazon approached Netflix about selling the company for a bargain-basement price. Netflix declined. Eventually, Netflix drove Blockbuster out of business and unleashed a global distribution model that changed how we watch TV forever.

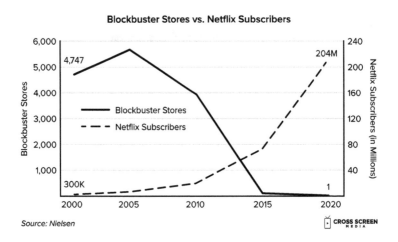

Blockbuster Stores vs. Netflix Subscribers

Source: Nielsen

Netflix founders Reed Hastings and Marc Randolph started with DVD rentals in **1997**, but within **3** years, they offered monthly subscriptions of at least **4** movies at a time with no return-by dates or late fees. By **2003**, they provided subscribers with algorithmic recommendations, and within **3** years, they had over **6M** subscribers. They made it easy for subscribers to find and rent movies they loved.

NETFLIX PIONEERS A NEW CATEGORY

In **2007**, Netflix launched "Watch Now," its streaming service.[40] It was a huge gamble: just over half of Americans (**53%**) had any type of broadband, and download speeds were not ready for video, even if it was primarily streamed on a PC. But Netflix invested **$40M** in developing the new streaming service and made a **thousand** movies available on demand to subscribers for free.[41] This was a bold bet for a service with fewer than **8M** subscribers in total.

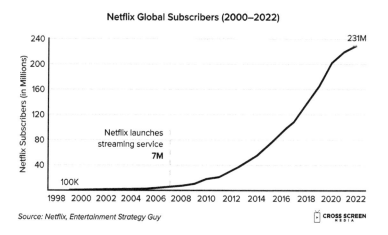

Netflix Global Subscribers (2000–2022)

Source: Netflix, Entertainment Strategy Guy

Still, a lot of competitors didn't take Netflix seriously. Blockbuster was the **first** company to make that mistake, but others followed. In **2010**, Jeffrey Bewkes—CEO of Time Warner (the parent company of HBO at the time)—was asked if he considered Netflix a threat. The streaming service's subscriber base had climbed from **8M** to **12M**, but Bewkes dismissed its potential.[42]

"It's a little bit like, is the Albanian army going to take over the world?" Bewkes told *The New York Times*, adding, "I don't think so."[43]

When Bewkes made this statement, there were only **18M** streaming TV households (**15%** of all households) in the US. Over the next decade, that number would grow to **103M** (↑**85M**), reaching **80%** of all households.

The shift to streaming TV had the wind at its back thanks to the **77M** households that added broadband internet from **2000** to **2010**.[44] By the end of the decade, only

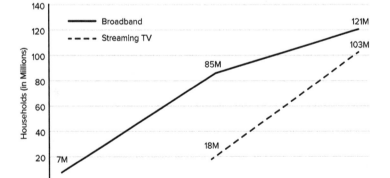

US Households with Broadband or Streaming (2000–2020)

1 out of every **5** households with broadband had started streaming, but that was about to change in a big way as more than **100M** households would be streaming by **2020**.

BECOMING HBO FASTER THAN HBO CAN BECOME NETFLIX

Competitors' indifference left many flat-footed when the streaming service took off. For example, in **2005**—2 years before Netflix started streaming content—HBO discussed doing the same thing but failed to act.[45] A year later, some HBO executives were pushing to buy Netflix, but again, HBO passed. Then, in **2013**, when Netflix launched *House of Cards*, the streaming service showed that it was capable of providing original content as good as that of HBO.[46]

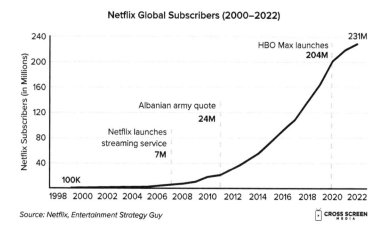

Netflix Global Subscribers (2000–2022)

Source: Netflix, Entertainment Strategy Guy

CROSS SCREEN MEDIA

▶ **WHY THIS MATTERS**

Over the course of a decade, Netflix built a global juggernaut while its competitors (HBO, Disney, etc.) ignored the changing market.

In **2013**, Netflix executive Ted Sarandos famously stated, "The goal is to become HBO faster than HBO can become us." A well-executed plan combined with baffling indifference from competitors made this a reality.

EIGHT

WILL THE LAST PERSON WITHOUT A STREAMING SERVICE PLEASE TURN OUT THE LIGHTS?

WALL STREET ROLLS OUT THE RED CARPET FOR STREAMING

If you had invested **$1K** in Netflix stock in **2003** and sold at the peak in **2021**, you'd have made a cool **$200K**.[47] The company's phenomenal growth from being an obscure DVD mail-order operator to the dominant streaming service with over **230M** subscribers has made it a darling of Wall Street.

Perhaps more than anything else, Netflix's ascension on Wall Street convinced a host of other streaming services to jump on the new entertainment bandwagon. Over the **13** years following Netflix's streaming launch in **2007**, there would be many new entrants, including:

1. Hulu (**2007**)
2. Amazon Prime Video (**2011**)
3. Paramount+ (originally CBS All Access, **2014**)
4. HBO Now (**2015**)
5. Apple TV+ (**2019**)
6. Disney+ (**2019**)
7. Peacock (**2020**)

Investors rewarded Netflix for spending lavishly on great new shows and producing a steady increase in subscribers, and the other streamers took note. They also noticed that it didn't matter that Netflix wasn't incredibly profitable; investors seemed to be prioritizing anticipated potential growth over current profitability.

An overarching question for the industry was how long this skewed prioritization would last. Then, in April **2022**, we got our answer when Netflix stock plunged **35%** after the streamer announced it had lost subscribers in the **first** quarter.

Suddenly, Wall Street had changed the rules of the game back to prioritizing profitability over growth. Maybe the halcyon days of lavish spending were coming to a close. Consequently, stock prices went up on news that streamers were reducing costs. They climbed again when Netflix announced a new ad-supported offering and a crackdown on shared passwords.

NEW BUSINESS MODELS EMERGE

Although Netflix has traditionally made money by selling subscriptions to its ad-free content, its recent addition of an ad-supported tier reflects the expanding ways streaming services try to make money. However, not everyone shares the same business model of subscriptions and/or ads. A few players in the streaming wars are investing **billions** of dollars to expand profits in another part of their business.

Three companies in particular—Amazon, Apple, and Disney)—are playing a different game.

Disney, for example, uses its media endeavors to cross-promote its retail and vacation businesses. Disney+ shows can help sell tickets to Disney World and Disneyland or help fill its cruise ships.

Apple, meanwhile, wants to sell its iPhones and MacBook Pro laptops, giving its customers a free year of streaming as an incentive to buy computer equipment. Apple doesn't talk much about its profits from streaming services, but it brags a lot about the quality of the shows it chooses. The company focuses on shows like *Ted Lasso*, which "have a reason for existing and may have a good message, and may make people feel better at the end of it," said CEO Tim Cook.[48]

Amazon wants customers to sign up for **$119**-per-year Amazon Prime memberships, so it dangles video- and music-streaming services as free benefits of membership. Amazon Prime Video also lets you rent or buy shows that you can't watch for free, bringing in a **few billion** dollars a year to Amazon.

▶ **WHY THIS MATTERS**

Consumption is shifting from linear TV to streaming, but not every streaming company follows the linear TV business model (ads, etc.). This shift will result in fewer ad impressions for advertisers over time.

. . . .

▶ **QUICK DEFINITION**

Ad Impressions: The individual occurrences of advertising content being displayed, whether or not it is viewed

. . . .

NINE

HOW WE WATCH TV TODAY

LINEAR TV IS STILL KING, BUT NOT FOR LONG

Linear TV still accounts for the majority (**56%**) of all TV viewing time, but over the long term, the trend is toward streaming. We already spend more time with streaming TV than broadcast or cable TV individually. The big question is when streaming will become the majority of viewers' time spent with TV. My prediction is **2026**.[49]

There are a few ways to look at this. Most households (**88%**) have at least **1** streaming device.[50] Second, the time viewers spend streaming is growing rapidly (↑ **38%** in **2022**). These **2** trends, combined with networks moving

Streaming Share of Total TV Time +101% since Start of Pandemic

December 2022: Total Day Persons 2+

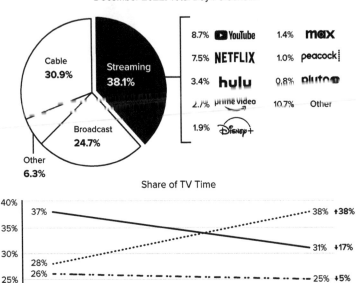

Share of TV Time

Source: Nielsen

Share of Time Spent Watching TV (2010–2025)

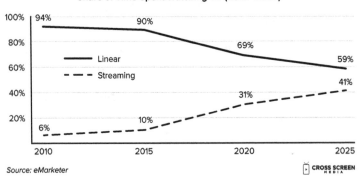

Source: eMarketer

their best content to streaming, lead me to be bullish about a rapid transition.

BILLIONS IN CONTENT SPEND DRIVE THE RAPID ADOPTION OF STREAMING

You'd think we would have run out of shows to watch on streaming by now. *Spoiler alert*: We haven't, thanks to **billions** of dollars in content spending from media companies fighting to capture our attention. Content spend in the US alone reached **$141B** in **2022**. With rising sports rights costs, this number is projected to grow to **$172B** by **2025**. According to Wells Fargo, Disney continued to lead the spending in **2023** with a **$35B** tab, followed by Warner Bros. Discovery (**$24B**), Netflix (**$20B**), Paramount+ (**$18B**), Amazon (**$15B**), and Apple TV+ (**$10B**).[51]

It is not just the expanding volume of shows leading to increased content costs. The shows themselves have never been so elaborate and expensive. It is now common to see a **1**-hour show cost **$20M+** per episode, and Amazon is smashing records by spending an estimated **$58M** per episode on *The Lord of the Rings: The Rings of Power*.[52]

On average, streaming companies lose **6%** of their customers every month due to churn.[53] This means a consumer stays with a streaming service for ~**17** months before

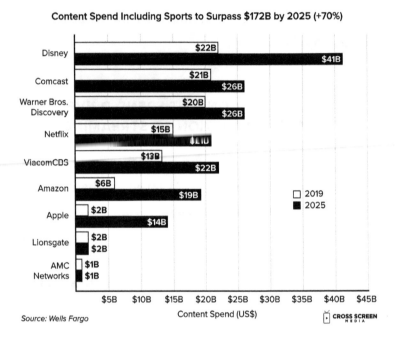

Content Spend Including Sports to Surpass $172B by 2025 (+70%)

Disney: $22B / $41B
Comcast: $21B / $26B
Warner Bros. Discovery: $20B / $26B
Netflix: $15B / $17B
ViacomCBS: $13B / $22B
Amazon: $6B / $19B
Apple: $2B / $14B
Lionsgate: $2B / $2B
AMC Networks: $1B / $1B

☐ 2019
■ 2025

Content Spend (US$)

$5B $10B $15B $20B $25B $30B $35B $40B $45B

Source: Wells Fargo

CROSS SCREEN MEDIA

canceling. For example, Netflix historically has had the lowest churn rate (**3%**) while Paramount+ has had the highest (**7%**).[54] This matters because Netflix and Paramount+ may spend roughly the same amount to acquire a new customer, but Netflix keeps that customer for **2X** longer (**30** months) vs. Paramount+ (**14** months).

▶ **QUICK DEFINITION**

Churn: A subscriber canceling their subscription
· ·

Streaming services need a steady influx of new shows to keep their subscribers. According to *The Wall Street Journal*, streaming services enjoy a surge of subscribers when they launch a new, highly hyped show or film. You saw it when Disney+ released *Hamilton* and HBO Max released *Wonder Woman 1984*. Each resulted in more than **400K** new sign-ups.[55]

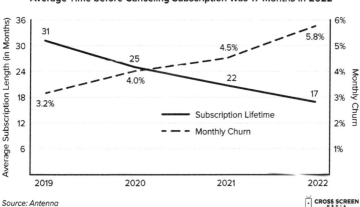

Average Time before Canceling Subscription Was 17 Months in 2022

Source: Antenna

This also explains why companies pay top dollar for "exclusive" content. They think fewer customers will cancel their subscriptions if the service has content that the consumer can't get anywhere else. For example, last Christmas, my kids (aka "Li'l Screens" and "Toddler Screens") wanted to watch *A Charlie Brown Christmas*. That show **first** aired in **1965** and has since been a holiday staple on linear TV for decades. But I couldn't find it listed anywhere. After a while, I realized that Apple TV+ had purchased exclusive streaming rights and that we'd need a subscription to watch.

TO BINGE OR NOT TO BINGE, THAT IS THE QUESTION

Netflix invented bingeing when it released the entire **first** season of *House of Cards* all at once. Subscribers could watch at their own pace, and viewers loved it. They could blow through a whole season of episodes in 1 sitting if they wanted to, rather than waiting around a week as each new episode was released, the way it would have been on HBO.

But bingeing didn't become the norm. Some streaming services, such as HBO Max, still dole out episodes every week rather than dropping an entire season all at once. Why?

When HBO starts airing widely popular shows like *Succession* and *The Last of Us*, with weekly releases, subscribers stick around. They keep coming back week after week. What HBO and other streamers fear is that they'll drop an entire season and watch in horror as viewers race through the episodes and then cancel their subscription until the next big show comes along.

Netflix, with its great wealth of shows, isn't as worried about that attrition, although it did a hybrid version of a show release with its popular *Ozark* series. It released half of the fourth season of *Ozark* in 1 cache of 7 shows and then released the second 7 shows months later. When the first half of Season **4** ended, Netflix auto-queued Season **1** of *Ozark*, and many viewers just sank back into the couch cushions to binge-rewatch the first **3** seasons as they waited for the series conclusion. Cagey move, Netflix.[56]

Netflix took a gamble with its *House of Cards* all-at-once distribution strategy, but it paid off. The show was a huge hit, and in the following years, Netflix's stock skyrocketed, and its subscriber base exploded. Today, people say binge-watching is **one** of the most appealing aspects of streaming.

The jury is still out as to whether other streamers will follow suit, particularly in light of the challenges Disney+ faced in retaining new customers who signed up for *Hamilton* and HBO encountered after *Wonder Woman*.

Binge-watching keeps the pressure on a network to have great shows lined up for when hits like *Ozark* and *House of Cards* are over, and that is what Netflix is trying to do when it spends **$17B** a year on new shows.

▶ **WHY THIS MATTERS**

Traditionally, watching TV shows live was necessary, but today, we watch them on demand and binge-watch entire seasons. Networks must continually release new content to maintain the attention of their audiences.

TEN

HOW WE WILL WATCH TV IN THE FUTURE

ALL TV WILL BE STREAMED

While many have predicted that linear TV will survive in some form for many years, other experts predict it will soon fade away altogether. Some give it as little as 3 years, while others see it hanging around, though they believe it will linger as a shadow of its former self.

"All TV is going to be streamed and therefore all TV advertising is going to be streamed," Roku executive Scott Rosenberg said. "This seems obvious today, but when we started saying it like **five, seven** years ago, people didn't believe us."[57]

With most entertainment shows migrating to streaming, many experts predict linear TV will soon lose its remaining scripted programs. In **2015**, during the prime-time hours of **0** p.m. to **11** p.m., the **4** major broadcast networks commanded around **30M** viewers combined. By **2022**, that number was down to **20M** (↓**33%**).[58] Still, as of **2023**, linear TV currently commands a larger share of total TV time than streaming.

The linear networks can thank news and sports for that. Consumers still enjoy watching live events on linear TV, and when major sporting events are available on both platforms, viewers prefer linear. The number of viewers who streamed the Super Bowl in **2022** doubled from the previous year (to **11M**), but the streaming audience was only **10%** of the total audience.

> ▶ **WHY THIS MATTERS**
>
> **90%** of viewers watched the **2022** Super Bowl via linear TV.

"People still like to sit down as a group in front of the TV," Warner Bros. Discovery executive Kathleen Finch told CNBC in early **2023**. "It's very communal."

News and sports will eventually head to streaming, but the economics may delay that move longer than many think. And, as I mentioned earlier, ESPN's lucrative deal with cable would be difficult to replicate on streaming.

ESPN is a must-carry for cable companies, and as a result, the all-sports network takes home **$658M** a month, which could not be made up right away through streaming subscriptions.

Local and national news programs are in the same boat: their economic model is based on broadcast and cable, and it's likely to stay that way until news departments can figure out how to generate significant advertising revenue from streaming news.

2022 was supposed to be the pivotal year when news divisions jumped into streaming. ABC News launched streaming content related to *Good Morning America*, as did NBC with its *Today* show. CBS News launched its streaming service with rotating anchors in New York, Los Angeles, and Washington, D.C.[59] ABC has its own live-streaming news service.

CNN had big plans for the launch of its **first** streaming service, CNN+. The streaming offering was launched while CNN was still under the AT&T umbrella, but when CNN ownership changed from AT&T to the newly created Warner Bros. Discovery, Inc., the new owners shut the service down after only a month because of the low number of viewers it attracted. Despite hiring big-name journalists like Chris Wallace, the **$5.99**-a-month CNN+ acquired fewer than **150K** subscribers in its first month compared to the **70M+** households who (indirectly) pay CNN through their pay-TV bundles.[60,61]

Despite the failure of CNN+, which many critics felt hadn't been given enough time to develop, many feel now will eventually embrace the streaming approach. Unlike sports, news already has close substitutes online that don't require a **$100**-per-month pay-TV subscription. For example, **70%+** of adults already get some of their news from social media.[62] If networks like CNN and Fox News don't create a robust offering through streaming, they risk losing that audience entirely.

GRANNY SCREENS AND THE CONFUSED CONSUMER

Last year, I bought my mother (aka "Granny Screens") a new Vizio TV. She watched most of her shows through a Roku plugged into her old TV, so I told her that all she had to do was plug her Roku into the new set, and she would get all her old channels and preferences. "It should be simple," I said. No need to connect the TV to the Wi-Fi. No need to create a new Vizio account. No need to go through any complicated setup. Just plug and play.

So she opened the box, turned on the TV, and followed the prompts on the screen. Then she called and started asking me questions: "What's the Wi-Fi password? Do I want this? Do I want that?"

I said, "Well, why do you need all that?"

And she said, "The TV is asking for it!"

Later, I realized what was going on. Vizio wanted Granny Screens to set up all her accounts through *them* and not Roku, because Vizio wants my mother to be *their* customer and not someone else's.

If she'd simply plugged in her Roku, Roku would continue to get a percentage of the ad revenue from the commercials my mother sees. Vizio wanted that business. Vizio also wanted to collect her viewing data and sell it to marketers eager to reach her.

> ▶ **KEY BATTLE IN THE SCREEN WARS**
>
> TV manufacturers no longer make money selling TVs. They sell TVs to sell advertising, which is how they make money. To run advertising, they need consumers to stream on their platform.

BEGUN, THE TVOS WARS HAVE

TVOS is the new world of streaming and TV advertising. Vizio is no longer in the business of *selling TVs* as much as it is in the business of *selling advertising*. Vizio makes

▶ **QUICK DEFINITION**

TVOS: TV operating system

· · · · · · · · · · · · · · ·

roughly **$0.05** in profit per **$1** it sells its TVs for.[63] That's not a great margin. But once Vizio has you as a customer, it makes **$0.70** for every **$1** of advertising it sells and delivers through its system This is 1 reason why the price of TVs is so low and continues to drop: The real money isn't in selling the TV. The real money is in the advertising pumped through the TV. TV makers want your eyeballs, so they make their TVs as affordable as possible.

How Does a Company Like Vizio Make Money?

Revenue Stream #1: Selling TVs

- **$300** per Smart TV
- **0.4%** Gross Profit
- **$1.17** Gross Profit per TV

Revenue Stream #2: Selling Advertising

- **$0.03** per SmartCast Hour
- **62.0%** Gross Profit
- **$0.02** Gross Profit per SmartCast Hour

Key Fact #1: Advertising becomes more valuable at **63** SmartCast hours.

Key Fact #2: The average household watches **21** SmartCast hours per week.

Source: Vizio company data

📺 CROSS SCREEN
MEDIA

With around **75%** of US homes equipped with smart TVs,[64] there is a huge market waiting to be tapped. That's why Vizio launched its in-house advertising unit in **2020** and is slashing TV prices. It's why Amazon started making TVs and selling them for less than the cost to make them.[65]

Eventually, buying video advertising from Roku, Vizio, LG, Samsung, or some other TV manufacturer will look like ad sales on Facebook or Google. The Facebook and Google advertising market produces **billions** of dollars in revenue for those companies, and as TV moves in that direction, there could be **millions** of advertisers in the US buying video ads who don't buy any video ads today.

TV makers don't have the right technology to do that—yet. Roku and Samsung both have ad-buying platforms, but they are early in their development instead of the closed-loop offering that I anticipate. This is the platform that we are building at Cross Screen Media, and we believe that it will be a game changer: all of your audiences, reporting, plans, and video-ad inventory in a single place, built specifically for local marketers.

But a great, affordable TV is not the only benefit of this deal. With streaming and smart TVs, consumers can set up their TVs just the way they want them, so they can find, watch, record, or replay whatever shows or programs they want. As the world around them follows a similar path, they'll find the content they want to be delivered to them with less searching. Their subscription services will know what they like and deliver it to them. They'll sit down, fire up the LG 55-incher, and view a personalized guide that gives them instant access to their favorite content, ordered by their preferences.

And the shows won't be the only thing personalized. So will the ads. Instead of seeing ads for trucks we'll never buy, we'll see ads for the destinations we want to travel to or for the shoe companies we patronize.

► WHY THIS MATTERS

All TV will eventually be streamed, but getting there will be a confusing fragmented mess.

. . . .

ELEVEN

PEAK TV AND OUR FRAGMENTED ATTENTION

CONTENT OPTIONS EXPLODE

The current age of TV—characterized by a large number of shows with high-quality subject matter and style—goes by a lot of names. Some call it "Peak TV" or "Prestige TV." It's also been called the "New," "**Second**," or "**Third** Golden Age of Television." There's some disagreement about when it began (and when it will reach its apex), but it's generally acknowledged to have started with the beginning of *The Sopranos* in **1999** and has continued with high-production-value shows like *The West Wing*, *The Wire*, *Friday Night Lights*, *Breaking Bad*, *Game of Thrones*, and *House of Cards*.

The number of scripted shows (comedies, dramas, and limited series), broadcast or streamed, has grown from 216 in 2010 to 599 in 2022 (↑177%).[66] This represents only a portion of all the shows on TV. It doesn't include unscripted shows, sports, news, many children's programs, and the growing market of non-English-language series.

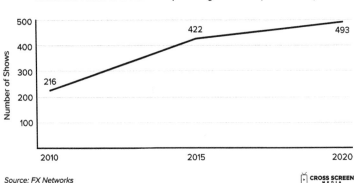

Estimated Number of Adult Scripted Original Series (2010–2020)

Source: FX Networks

As discussed in Chapter 9, the land grab for streaming led to an increase in content spend, which led to an explosion in the number of shows. New networks that were never distributed through broadcast or cable popped up with the arrival of Netflix, Disney+, Peacock, and others, and these new networks all wanted to offer a full slate of shows. An estimated **50%** of Netflix's scripted shows are original content, and even streamers like Disney+ and Peacock, which have ties to cable and broadcast channels, now produce shows exclusively for streaming.[67] You can't find a show like *The Mandalorian* anywhere but on the Disney+ streaming service.

The growth of shows was also indicative of the race among the top streaming services to increase subscriptions while decreasing churn. But now investors expect streaming services to start generating a profit, and that may curtail the overall investment in new shows. For consumers, this will mean higher monthly subscription prices for streaming services with fewer shows. For advertisers, the higher subscription price will make ad-supported plans more appealing, which will lead to greater reach for streaming ads and an overall increase in inventory.

NUMBER OF SHOWS GROWS
FASTER THAN TIME WITH TV

Despite these new shows, our time spent with TV has not grown much. In fact, between **2010** and **2025**, the average time we spend watching convergent TV is estimated to grow by only **3** minutes (↑**1%**).

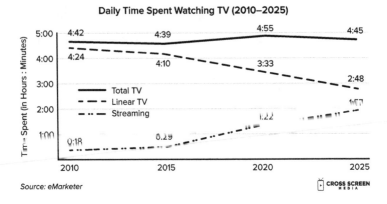

Daily Time Spent Watching TV (2010–2025)

Source: eMarketer

The bottom line is that we have roughly the same amount of attention (~**5** hours/day) being spread over **3X** as much TV content. If you, as a consumer, feel overwhelmed by the fragmentation of watching TV, consider how the media companies feel. They are spending more money to chase a fraction of the audience (↓**63%**), which leads to even greater challenges for advertisers, as media plans that previously were a few line items long can now span multiple pages!

THE GRID NO LONGER MATTERS

Before streaming, TV networks had a limited number of time slots to fill. They had morning news shows, midmorning talk shows, afternoon soap operas, and primetime evening shows from **8** to **11** p.m.

Total Time Spent Watching TV Is Flat

+7%	+185%	+7%	−63%
Time Spent Watching Video	Number of Original Shows	TV Households	Time per Show

Estimated Number of Adult Scripted Original Series

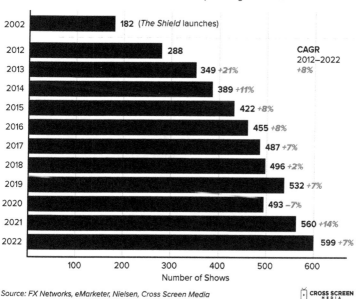

Year	Number of Shows
2002	182 (*The Shield* launches)
2012	288
2013	349 +21%
2014	389 +11%
2015	422 +8%
2016	455 +8%
2017	487 +7%
2018	496 +2%
2019	532 +7%
2020	493 −7%
2021	560 +14%
2022	599 +7%

CAGR 2012–2022 +8%

Source: FX Networks, eMarketer, Nielsen, Cross Screen Media

CROSS SCREEN MEDIA

Streaming doesn't face the same constraints. Streaming services don't have lineups. They have libraries with unlimited shelf space to display their shows. The sheer volume of shows creates a bit of a "discovery problem": viewers can get lost in choices. However, streaming has responded with playlists, recommendation engines, and free, ad-supported television (FAST) channels. FAST channels (like Pluto TV and Peacock) combine streaming shows in a linear format similar to a cable or satellite programming guide. FAST channels are growing rapidly and make the choices for you, without requiring a streaming subscription or a pay-TV package.

In a world with thousands of shows, movies, and live events, streaming programs are now judged based on minutes viewed and subscriber retention. After assessing shows according to the number of unique accounts that viewed a title, Netflix has shifted to measuring the collective number of hours viewers spend watching each title.

In Part **II**, I will walk through the history of TV advertising and how it will work in the future.

▶ WHY THIS MATTERS

For advertisers to reach their target audience, they need to advertise on more TV shows than ever. This will only grow more challenging as more consumption shifts to streaming.

. . . .

HOW TV ADVERTISING WILL WORK IN THE FUTURE

TWELVE

A BRIEF HISTORY OF TV ADVERTISING

FROM 0 TO $70B

I discussed the **first** TV ad in the introduction—the **10**-second spot for Bulova that only a **few thousand** people saw before a baseball game. Television advertising took shape rapidly after that **first** Bulova ad. Gimbels department store and Firestone Tire started running ads, and after World War II—as the percentage of homes with TVs grew from less than **1%** in **1940** to over **9%** by **1950** —big brands like Kraft, Colgate, and GE became program sponsors, with some control of the content of the shows they funded.[68] Westinghouse, for example, sponsored *The*

Adventures of Ozzie and Harriet and ensured that many scenes were shot in the kitchen, where the brand's shiny appliances were on full display. Live commercials, such as John Cameron Swayze demonstrating the durability of Timex watches, were common.[69]

By **1960**, TV advertisers could reach **90%** of all US households, something no other medium could match. Although expensive, TV advertising became what *Forbes* magazine called the "default business solution" for most ad agencies. In the TV show *Mad Men*, which followed the life and times of a Madison Avenue agency in the '60s, TV advertising was a small portion of Don Draper's universe. Soon, however, TV would become the dominant medium. Not only did it provide impressive reach, it also delivered metrics and measurable results, making it easier for ad agencies to find target audiences based on Nielsen ratings.

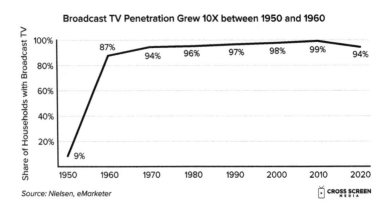

Broadcast TV Penetration Grew 10X between 1950 and 1960

Source: Nielsen, eMarketer

When VCRs became popular in the late **1970s** and viewers could record shows and fast-forward through commercials, some predicted the collapse of TV advertising. It didn't happen. It also didn't happen when digital video recorders (DVRs) and TiVo arrived **20** years later. Some predicted most households would adopt recording technology, but by **2015**, penetration for TiVo and other devices was only **40%**, and even those who had it preferred live TV over recorded programs. Even those watching recorded programs often don't skip the ads. By **1** estimate, people only fast-forward through **5–8%** of all ads.[70]

As adoption soared, so did the amount of money advertisers invested in TV. In **1950**, TV earned **$171M** (**$2B** in **2022** dollars) in ad revenue. Ten years later, it had grown **10X**.[71]

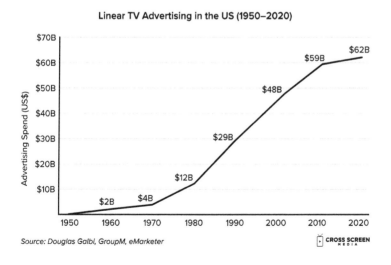

Linear TV Advertising in the US (1950–2020)

Source: Douglas Galbi, GroupM, eMarketer

By **2020**, advertisers were spending **$62B** on linear TV ads in the US.

According to *Insider Intelligence*, linear TV ad spend in the US peaked in **2022** at **$67B** and is expected to decline to just under **$57B** (↓**15%**) by **2027**.[72] Experts see this change as a result of viewers shifting their consumption from linear to streaming TV—and believe the ad dollars will likely follow them. In **2022**, for instance, all forms of digital video advertising (streaming, mobile, and desktop) hit **$74B**—surpassing linear TV advertising for the **first** time.

SHIFT TO STREAMING ADVERTISING BEGINS

Advertising on linear TV may have peaked in **2022** at **$67B**, but convergent TV advertising is still growing, driven by streaming TV. The entire convergent TV advertising market will approach **$100B** by **2027**.

▶ **QUICK DEFINITION**

Convergent TV Advertising:
Linear TV advertising +
Streaming TV advertising

The rise in streaming advertising represents a big shift from a few years ago, when major services like Netflix were ad-free. Netflix executives vowed for years never to accept advertising—until in **2023**, favorable economics and pressure from investors persuaded the

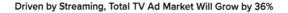

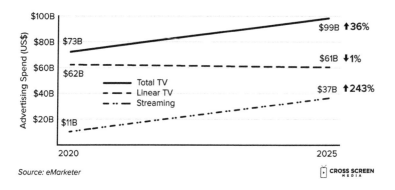

Driven by Streaming, Total TV Ad Market Will Grow by 36%

Advertising Spend (US$)

- Total TV
- Linear TV
- Streaming

$73B
$62B
$11B

$99B ↑36%
$61B ↓1%
$37B ↑243%

2020 — 2025

Source: eMarketer

CROSS SCREEN MEDIA

company to start offering a less expensive, ad-supported subscription for those who didn't want to pay full price.

Now HBO Max, Disney+, and other subscription streamers are rolling out ad-supported options as well, joining Peacock, Pluto TV, Tubi, and others.

The shift in consumer attention toward streaming is underway, and advertisers are hungry to get their products in front of this audience. By **2025**, an esti-

▶ WHY THIS MATTERS

As consumption shifts to streaming, advertising dollars will follow. In the future, streaming advertising will replace linear TV in much the same way that linear TV replaced radio.

mated **41%** of our convergent TV time will be spent with streaming, but it will only account for **36%** of ad spend. This allocation will flip as a higher share of streaming time becomes ad-supported.

It's not hard to see the trend here. Viewers are dropping cable in droves and flocking to streaming. As more viewers develop "subscription fatigue," it's likely that the cheaper, ad-supported platforms will continue to draw larger audiences. Those viewers will still be scattered across **thousands** of shows and many screens at all hours of the day, but if advertisers can find the viewers they want, chances are good they'll get an ad in front of their target audience.

▶ **WHY THIS MATTERS**

It took linear TV advertising 70+ years to peak, and streaming has just gotten started. The US convergent TV ad market will reach **$100B** within a few years.

82

THIRTEEN

HOW LARGE IS THE CONVERGENT TV ADVERTISING MARKET?

THE CONVERGENT TV AD MARKET

Ad spending on convergent TV—the combination of linear TV with streaming TV—is growing. In **2020**, total spending reached **$73B**, with more than **$62B** (**85%**) going to linear TV. By **2025**, that total is expected to reach **$91B**, with the amount going to linear declining to **$59B** (**64%**). In other words, the portion of the total market for streaming TV advertising will grow from essentially **0%** in

2015 to 36% in **2025**. All the growth in TV ad spending will come from the streaming side.

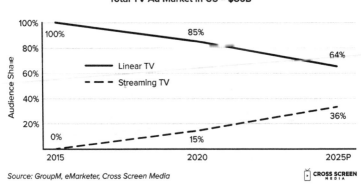

Total TV Ad Market in US = $86B

Source: GroupM, eMarketer, Cross Screen Media

WHERE DOES TV FIT IN THE OVERALL ADVERTISING MARKET?

One of the main reasons I can write an entire book around a single ad category (convergent TV advertising) is simply because of how *large* the category is. Convergent TV advertising accounts for **1** out of every **4** advertising dollars spent in the US.[73]

The TV ad industry is diverse, with many different ways to

▶ **WHY THIS MATTERS**

Streaming accounts for all of the growth in convergent TV advertising. Projected change in convergent TV spend between **2015** and **2025**:

- Streaming TV: ↑**$33B**
- Linear TV: ↓**$10B**

classify spend. If we look at these classifications, it becomes obvious that a few—such as streaming TV and targeted

1 in 4 Advertising Dollars Goes to TV

Total (2022): $305 billion

TV
28%

Non-TV
72%

Source: GroupM, eMarketer, Cross Screen Media

CROSS SCREEN
MEDIA

▶ **WHY THIS MATTERS**

All TV advertising is becoming targeted and will be streamed.

Streaming TV Is the Fastest-Growing Segment of TV Advertising

TV Ad Segment	2022 (US$)	2027 (US$)	Change	CAGR
Streaming	$20B	$40B	+$20B	+15%
Targeted	$37B	$72B	+$34B	+14%
Total	$87B	$97B	+$10B	+2%
Linear	$67B	$57B	−$10B	−3%
Non-Targeted	$50B	$26B	−$24B	−12%

Source: GroupM, eMarketer, Cross Screen Media

CROSS SCREEN
MEDIA

TV—are driving the overall growth. Likewise, a few categories are declining, such as nontargeted TV advertising (age, gender, demo, etc.).

1M VIDEO ADVERTISERS

Today, more than **90%** of advertising on national network television is purchased by only about **250** brands.[74] The costs are too high for most brands, and the audience is so broad as to make any kind of message too general to have much effect. As a result, we see a lot of ads for insurance companies, fast food, miracle medications, and trucks from Chevy, Ford, and Toyota.

That group is minuscule compared to the overall number of video advertisers in the US. Since **2020**, the amount spent on digital video advertising has grown from **$43B** to **$109B**, powered by more than **1M** video advertisers. To

Local Has ~1M Video Advertisers

	Advertising Spend (US$)	Number of Advertisers	Spend per Advertiser
Linear TV Only	$8.6B	77K	$111K
All Video	$18.2B	137K	$133K
CTV/Mobile/Desktop Only	$17.6B	814K	$22K

Source: Borrell Associates, Cross Screen Media

CROSS SCREEN MEDIA

put this into perspective, for every **single** national network TV advertiser, there are **5K** digital video advertisers in the US that don't buy national network TV advertising.[75]

▶ **WHY THIS MATTERS**

Streaming TV advertising has no barriers to entry. All **1M+** advertisers (mostly local) can bid on the same inventory as the largest national brands.

FOURTEEN

HOW CONVERGENCE WILL CHANGE TV ADVERTISING

THE ECONOMICS OF LINEAR TV ADVERTISING

Today, each hour of linear TV (with ads) that a consumer watches generates **$0.27** per hour in advertising revenue. This number is extremely important and worth unpacking, especially as networks and advertisers increasingly need to make comparisons to streaming economics.

In **2022**, iSpot estimated there were **8B** linear TV ad impressions. I combine that number with our market estimate for linear TV ad spend of **$67B** to get **$8** as an average CPM.[76] The final step is to apply an average ad load for linear TV, which I set at **16** minutes or **32** individual spots.

Linear TV Networks Generate $0.27/Hour in Advertising Revenue

Assumption	
Linear TV Ad Impressions (2022)	8B
Linear TV Ad Market (2022)	$66.7B
CPM for Linear TV	$8
Ad Minutes per Hour	16
30-Second Spots per Hour	32
Ad Revenue per Hour	$0.27

Source: iSpot, eMarketer, GroupM, Cross Screen Media

CROSS SCREEN
MEDIA

▶ **QUICK DEFINITION**

Cost Per Mille (CPM): The cost per **1K** ad impressions, an industry-standard measure for selling ads, calculated as (Total Cost ÷ Impressions) × **1,000**

One item that surprises people is the relatively low average CPM (**$8**) for linear TV. It is surprising because most of what we read focuses on the CPM for high-value inventory such as local news (**$25**), primetime (**$47**), and sports (**$70**).[77] With linear TV, there can be up to an **8X** shift in pricing between less desirable networks/dayparts and the most in-demand shows. This range has less to do with the target audience and more to do with content adjacency and total reach. When we look at streaming, some of these trends will start to flip.

CPMs for Sports Are ~8X Higher Than Average for Linear TV

Content Type	CPM	Ad Minutes per Hour	30-Second Spots	Ad Revenue per Hour
Sports	$70	16.0	32	$2.24
Primetime Broadcast	$47	16.0	32	$1.50
Local Broadcast News	$25	16.0	32	$0.80
Average Linear TV	$8	16.0	32	$0.26
Everything Else	< $8	16.0	32	< $0.26

Source: Wells Fargo, Cross Screen Media

CROSS SCREEN MEDIA

THE ECONOMICS OF STREAMING TV ADVERTISING

For streaming with ads, each hour a person watches generates **$0.24** in advertising revenue. Out of the gate, an hour of ad-supported linear TV generates **11%** more

Streaming TV Networks (with Ads) Generate
$0.24 per Hour in Advertising Revenue

Assumption	
Streaming TV Ad Impressions (2022)	1B
Streaming TV Ad Market (2022)	$20B
CPM for Streaming TV	$30
Ad Minutes per Hour	4
30-Second Spots per Hour	8
Ad Revenue per Hour	$0.24

Source: The Hollywood Reporter, Cheddar News, Cross Screen Media

CROSS SCREEN MEDIA

revenue than streaming TV. In the long term, though, I anticipate this disparity will flip, and streaming TV will generate a significantly higher revenue per hour.

Streaming TV also has premium inventory that commands higher CPMs, such as Netflix (**$45**) and Disney+ (**$40**).[78]

Netflix Would Generate $0.36 per Hour in Advertising Revenue at $45 CPM

Network	CPM	Ad Minutes per Hour	30-Second Spots	Ad Revenue per Hour
Disney+	$40	6	12	$0.48
Paramount+	$23	10	20	$0.46
NETFLIX	$45	4	8	$0.36
max	$40	4	8	$0.32
peacock	$30	5	10	$0.30
Average Streaming TV	$30	4	8	$0.24

Source: Digiday, Business Insider, The Hollywood Reporter

CROSS SCREEN MEDIA

One difference with streaming is that the highest-demand programming only commands a **2X** premium over the average. This creates an interesting dilemma for the entertainment industry as a whole. On the one hand, streaming TV and linear TV already generate similar advertising revenue per hour (**$0.24** vs. **$0.27**). On the other hand, the most premium content on linear TV—sports and primetime—generates 2X to 4X the advertising revenue per hour as the top streaming network (Netflix).

Linear TV Dominates Top Spots for Ad Revenue per Hour

Content Type	CPM	Ad Minutes per Hour	30-Second Spots	Ad Revenue per Hour
Linear: Sports	$70	16	32	$2.24
Linear: Primetime	$47	16	32	$1.50
Linear: Local News	$25	16	32	$0.80
Streaming: Disney+	$40	6	12	$0.48
Streaming: Paramount+	$23	10	20	$0.46
Streaming: Netflix	$45	4	8	$0.36
Streaming: Max	$40	4	8	$0.32
Streaming: Peacock	$30	5	10	$0.30
Average Linear TV	$8	16	32	$0.26
Average Streaming TV	$30	4	8	$0.24

Source: Wells Fargo, Digiday, Business Insider,
The Hollywood Reporter, Cross Screen Media

CROSS SCREEN
MEDIA

WHY STREAMING TV IS BETTER

Today, streaming is already better for advertisers based on efficiency, due to its targeting and measurement capabilities, but it lacks the overall scale for reach that linear TV offers. The scale of streaming will grow dramatically as the compounding effects of A) a greater share of TV time going to streaming and B) a larger share of ad-supported streaming subscribers.

Remember, eventually, **100%** of TV will be streamed, leading to **100%** of TV advertising being streamed. This massive shift will be a win for all sides (networks, Wall Street, etc.), since I firmly believe the streaming TV advertising market will be larger than today's linear TV market.

The growth in streaming TV advertising is driven partially by the shift in overall consumption, but that is far from the only reason.

> ▶ **WHY THIS MATTERS**
>
> Streaming TV is a game changer for local advertisers because they get the added benefit of hyperlocal geotargeting.

Streaming TV advertising is also growing because it is flat-out better for ~**99%** of the **1M** video advertisers in the US.

Key advantages of streaming TV:

1. Audience targeting
2. Geographic targeting
3. Measurement
4. Low minimums

Advantage #1: Streaming TV advertising is addressable by nature since it is delivered at the impression level. Impression-level delivery allows advertisers to pay different prices for impressions that reach different households.

For example, a local car dealership is willing to pay a premium to reach a household in the market for a new car. This is a major difference from linear TV sold at the spot level. Buying at the spot level requires that the advertiser pay the same amount for each impression, whether they are a target or not.

> **QUICK DEFINITION**
>
> **Addressable Advertising:** The targeting of a specific audience (auto intenders, swing voters, etc.) on a **1:1** basis, at either the household or the individual level

Advantage #2: The ability to target a specific audience is a major advantage for streaming TV, which turns into a game-changer when combined with geographic targeting. The same advertiser who is trying to reach a household that is in the market for a new car can also restrict that ad to a certain radius (**20** miles, etc.) from their business.

For example, a local car dealership in Athens, Georgia, currently pays an eCPM of **$813** on linear TV to reach a potential car buyer who lives within **20** miles of the dealership. An advertiser trying to reach potential car buyers from anywhere in the United States would have

> **QUICK DEFINITION**
>
> **Effective CPM (eCPM):** The effective cost per **1K** impressions, calculated as CPM ÷ (Viewability %) ÷ (On-Target %); for digital ads, this means on-target, viewable, **5**-second views

▶ **QUICK DEFINITION**

Ad Viewability: An advertising metric that quantifies how much of an ad is actually seen; for video ads, there is a range of industry standards with minimums as low as 2 seconds (at Cross Screen Media, we use a minimum of 5 seconds before we consider an ad watched)

· ·

an eCPM of **$80**. As we move to a streaming environment where every ad is targetable at the household level, we will see that local advertisers will pay **10X** as much for impressions that hit the correct target.

Case Study: Car Dealership in Athens, GA

Audience	House-holds	% of Market	eCPM Linear TV	Streaming TV
Adults in Atlanta Market	2.5M	100%	$20	$35
Above + 30-Mile Radius	206K	8%	$274	$55
Above + Auto Intender	51K	2%	$813	$75

Source: Cross Screen Media

CROSS SCREEN MEDIA

Advantage #3: Streaming TV is built on similar technology (ad servers, etc.) as digital video, which allows for granular measurement. An advertiser can track the basics, such as impressions, clicks, and time spent, while combining this data with more performance-based metrics, such as

Measure Reach and Frequency for All Your Video Advertising

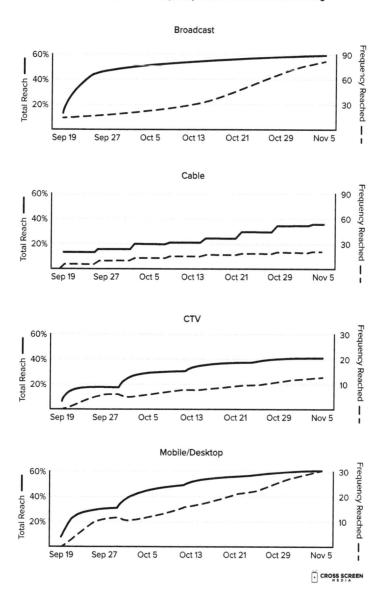

▶ **QUICK DEFINITIONS**

Ad Frequency: The average number of times households or individuals view an advertisement during a specific time period

Ad Reach: The total number of different individuals or households exposed, at least once, to an advertisement during a given period

Reach Percentage: The percentage of individuals or households exposed, calculated as (# of Individuals Reached) ÷ (# of Individuals in the Total Audience)

. . . .

deduplicated reach/frequency, in-store visits, and website purchases.

Advantage #4: Since streaming TV can be bought at the impression level, there are low barriers to entry. Advertisers can develop small campaigns with multiple audiences and video-ad creatives for a test-and-learn approach. Once they identify the best-performing audiences and ad creatives, they can increase their financial investment.

▶ **WHY THIS MATTERS**

Unlike linear TV, streaming TV advertising has multiple advantages. Local advertisers benefit from these advantages more than national advertisers do. As a result, local advertisers will adopt streaming advertising faster than their national counterparts.

. . . .

FIFTEEN

THE VIDEO ADVERTISER OF THE FUTURE

AGNOSTIC BETWEEN LINEAR AND STREAMING TV

Today, almost every local advertiser I meet with is working toward being agnostic between linear and streaming TV. They want what is best for their clients (brands, nonprofits, political campaigns, etc.), and that is shifting daily toward streaming. To be "screen agnostic," they need unbiased information that helps them split their spending between linear and streaming TV.

Most people watch some of both and are reachable with advertising through either. The challenge is choosing the right balance.

The other challenge for marketers is the fact that linear and streaming use different metrics to measure results. As previously discussed, streaming ads measure cost per 1K impressions (CPM), while linear TV reports gross rating points (GRP), measuring what percentage of the audience actually saw your ad. They are completely different metrics.

▶ **QUICK DEFINITION**

Gross Rating Points (GRP): The "total audience" exposure to advertising messages; **1** GRP is equivalent to the number of views where, on average, **1%** of the total (not target) audience has seen an ad **1** time

· ·

But when there is a single platform for planning and measuring both linear and streaming, this problem goes away. Our company has already worked out a way to put everything into a common currency, which can cut both ways. We can convert gross rating points to effective cost per **1K** (eCPM), and we

Viewing Digital as TV and TV as Digital

Targeted Rating Points (TRP)

Effective Cost per Thousand (eCPM)

CROSS SCREEN MEDIA

can convert eCPM into targeted rating points. Our software allows you to compare an ad running on linear to the same ad on streaming and see how the 2 media match up.

THE VIDEO ADVERTISING
PLATFORM OF THE FUTURE

Even though all TV will eventually be streamed, that future is still a ways off. When the NFL signed a new 10-year contract to broadcast its games on linear TV, it ensured that linear TV would continue to run side by side with streaming TV until at least 2032. That means many advertisers will continue to straddle the linear and streaming realms and buy ad space in both.

It also means buying ad space and measuring the effectiveness of each platform will continue to be a complicated process. Placing streaming ads will require advertisers to work through a demand-side platform (DSP) or something similar to choose their slots and schedule ads. For linear, they will have to use a completely different platform, and they'll likely have to negotiate with a human to set up their ads. This is a far cry from ad platforms like Facebook and Google, where advertisers can plan, activate, and measure their advertising against audience data with 1 log-in. The downside to these "walled gardens" is that you can only

► **QUICK DEFINITION**

Demand-Side Platform (DSP): a system in which advertisers buying digital advertising inventory can activate and manage campaigns across hundreds of publishers aggregated into a single interface; DSPs also allow advertisers to adjust campaigns midflight instead of having to wait until the campaign has concluded

see metrics for their specific inventory (Facebook, YouTube, etc.), which does not help with the other 95%+ of your convergent TV buy.

Soon, that kind of tool will emerge for television, making it much easier to buy advertising on the big screen. The ideal world will be a closed-loop video-advertising platform like Facebook's, which you can use to plan, activate, and measure 100% of your convergent TV buy with a single log-in.

Harness the Power of CTV and Local TV

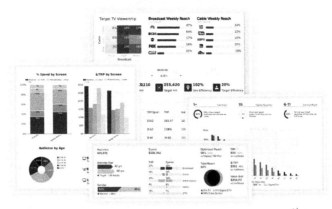

Source: Cross Screen Media's ScreenSolve platform

CROSS SCREEN MEDIA

THE 3 PHASES OF SHIFTING TO CONVERGENT TV

Convergent TV advertising will be the dominant trend into the **2030s,** and future-proofing your business will take time and practice. Some advertisers will start with a strong background in linear TV, while others may only know streaming. Either way, streaming TV is the future, and being able to offer all forms of TV advertising together is what your customers want.

A common path for media buying agencies to shift to convergent TV looks like this:

- **Phase 1**: Both linear and streaming TV advertising are offered by the same company (agency, etc.).
- **Phase 2**: A single team within a company develops a deep understanding of both.
- **Phase 3**: Individuals within teams develop a deep understanding of both.

▶ **QUICK DEFINITION**

Media Buying (aka "Activation"): A method that marketing agencies apply after a media planner completes their research and builds a campaign strategy; media buyers use this strategy to find and bid on ad inventory across multiple ad channels

. . . .

▶ **WHY THIS MATTERS**

The video advertiser of the future will buy all forms of TV advertising together, utilizing rich audience data rather than proxies such as age or gender demographics.

. . . .

In Part III, I will walk through our playbook for winning the future of attention with convergent TV.

PART

3

WINNING THE BATTLE FOR ATTENTION WITH CONVERGENT TV

SIXTEEN

WHAT CAN POLITICAL CAMPAIGNS TEACH US?

Successful US political campaigns have been masters of local advertising since the **first** time Americans cast a vote. With the **1952** launch of Eisenhower's "I Like Ike" TV ads (produced by Disney employees and managed by the worldwide ad agency BBDO), video advertising quickly became a dominant channel for political messaging. Since then, **tens of billions** of dollars have been spent across TV and video channels to persuade, engage, and mobilize voters. The high stakes, required speed, and emphasis on hyperlocal targeting make political campaigns a strong teacher for local advertisers across any industry.

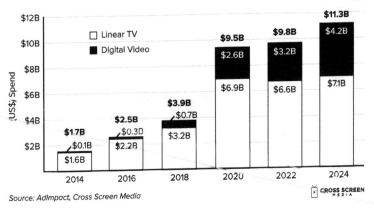

Source: AdImpact, Cross Screen Media

Political campaigns are a special breed for multiple reasons, including the following:

- They start over every **2 to 4** years.
- Almost **100%** of political donations are spent by election day—no saving for a rainy day.
- **80%** of political ad spending is concentrated in an **8**-week period every **2** years.
- Regardless of their investment, **second**-place finishers earn no market share!

Despite these differences, political campaigns have the same goal as any organization buying local TV and streaming advertising: reaching a specific target audience as efficiently and effectively as possible in an increasingly fragmented media universe. Political campaigns continue to be at the forefront of developing highly effective, highly targeted campaigns.

The key lessons for convergent TV advertisers to draw from politics are:

1. Your true audience must be at the center of your planning.
2. All campaigns start local.
3. Constantly test, learn, and improve—or fall behind.

YOUR TRUE AUDIENCE MUST BE AT THE CENTER OF YOUR PLANNING

When it comes to successful political campaigns, understanding your audience is everything. For example, in the upcoming **2024** election cycle, I project only **14%** of voters (**12%** of adults)—roughly **31M** people— are up for grabs as undecided voters. Most of the **$11B** campaigns that will spend on video advertising will target this audience, at an average of **$364** per persuadable voter.

The 2024 Video Advertisement Battleground
$11B in Video Advertising Targets 31M Persuadable Voters in 2023–2024

	Individuals	Video Ad Spend per Individual
US 18+ Population	258M	$44
Above + Registered to Vote	220M	$51
Above + Likely to Vote	155M	$73
Above + Persuadable	31M	$364

Source: AdImpact, Cross Screen Media (Sept 2023)   CROSS SCREEN MEDIA

ALL CAMPAIGNS START LOCAL

Political campaigns understand how crucial it is to target distinct geographic areas. Candidates don't want to advertise to anyone outside their voting district. It's a waste of money because those people can't legally vote in that candidate's election, no matter how many ads they see.

For most advertisers, this geotargeting doesn't have to be so precise. Nevertheless, if you are a regional bank, a local auto dealer, or a hospital center, your business has a distinct geographic footprint. Any spending outside that footprint goes to customers who are likely to patronize other businesses closer to home.

CONSTANTLY TEST, LEARN, AND
IMPROVE—OR FALL BEHIND

In December 2007, Democratic presidential candidate Barack Obama trailed the frontrunners by double digits. To help voters learn more about the candidate, Obama's director of analytics, Dan Siroker, tried several combinations of images or videos with 4 different buttons on Obama's landing page. In total, the campaign had 24 different test combinations to determine which best engaged website visitors.[79]

Every visitor to the candidate's splash page was randomly shown 1 of the combinations, and the campaign tracked how many went on to sign up. The buttons said "SIGN UP," "SIGN UP NOW," "LEARN MORE," or "JOIN US NOW," and the images included 3 videos of Obama in action and 3 still photographs, including a portrait of the candidate and his family and another of Obama on the campaign trail.

Before conducting the experiment, Obama staffers favored 1 video over all the others. Siroker said choosing that video—or the other 2 videos, for that matter—would have been a "huge mistake." The experiment showed that the most effective combination was the playful family portrait with the "LEARN MORE" button. The campaign's original splash page had an **8%** sign-up rate, but the new combination had a **12%** sign-up rate.

That **50%** increase in sign-ups meant that over the course of the campaign, Obama attracted nearly **3M** additional email addresses. When the campaign emailed those supporters to request that they volunteer, it converted about **10%**. That meant that by testing the right combination of visuals and language, the campaign brought in **288K** additional donors. With each supporter who signed up donating an average of **$21**, the campaign generated an additional **$60M** in donations.

Testing and learning from linear TV ads, where it can take months to see if your **30**-second ad increased sales, is difficult and expensive. Streaming provides actionable data in real time, allowing marketers to make a larger variety of ads and test them across various networks to identify the best options. Marketers can then pinpoint who they reached within the target frequency range. With this data, media planners can confidently adjust the dials on budget allocation across screen type, network, and daypart to make the most of the campaign before it concludes.

The use of advanced data and analytics in **2024** will make past elections look as outdated as Henry Ford's Model T. Groundbreaking technologies such as machine learning and artificial intelligence will allow campaigns to slice and dice the electorate in a myriad of ways. Streaming TV advertising was built from the ground up to take full advantage of these advancements, and I anticipate it will be ground zero for campaigns as the first Tuesday in November 2024 approaches.

▶ **WHY THIS MATTERS**

Convergent TV will be ground zero for winning political campaigns in **2024**. Smart political campaigns offer a glimpse into the future. Local advertisers will focus on cutting-edge tactics and strategies around audience data and media consumption.

SEVENTEEN

DOING IT RIGHT (CASE STUDIES)

The years of delivering broadly themed messages to a mass audience have given way to more precise messages aimed at people most interested in what you have to say. But how does that play out in today's real world, when potential customers are scattered across a variety of screens with endless content options to watch? The following case studies illustrate how advertisers leverage the crucial mix of technology and expertise to maximize the impact of each campaign.

CASE STUDY 1
REACHING HEALTHCARE CONSUMERS

Challenge

Healthcare systems are more complex than ever, and consumers have been overwhelmed by messages about new drugs and treatments for an ever-increasing number of conditions. Healthcare advertisers need to reach the right consumer with the right message, while still safeguarding patients' privacy and protected health information (PHI).

An agency working with a local healthcare center needed to advertise lines of service in 2 different media markets. This agency traditionally used a single media allocation across target markets, but with heightened budget pressure, they needed to increase the on-target reach of campaigns without increasing advertising spending. The agency turned to Cross Screen Media to maximize the impact.

Solution

With an analysis of the media consumption habits and geographic distribution of the target audience, the agency realized that using a media allocation for 1 market would incur significant waste in the other. Instead, they worked with Cross Screen Media to create a market-by-market plan to optimize on-target reach. As shown in the chart below, Market A's audience has much higher engagement with ads served over cable TV and mobile or desktop video, meaning a plan with a heavy emphasis on those channels would miss a large percentage of the same audience in Market B.

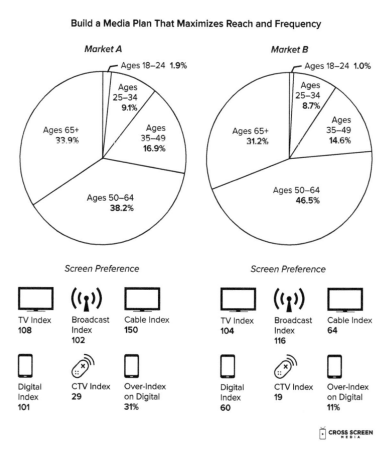

Build a Media Plan That Maximizes Reach and Frequency

Market A

- Ages 18–24 1.9%
- Ages 25–34 9.1%
- Ages 35–49 16.9%
- Ages 50–64 38.2%
- Ages 65+ 33.9%

Market B

- Ages 18–24 1.0%
- Ages 25–34 8.7%
- Ages 35–49 14.6%
- Ages 50–64 46.5%
- Ages 65+ 31.2%

Screen Preference

TV Index 108
Broadcast Index 102
Cable Index 150
Digital Index 101
CTV Index 29
Over-Index on Digital 31%

Screen Preference

TV Index 104
Broadcast Index 116
Cable Index 64
Digital Index 60
CTV Index 19
Over-Index on Digital 11%

CROSS SCREEN MEDIA

Additionally, geotargeting helped the agency direct ads only to the target audience within the healthcare center's geographic footprint. The map below shows how the healthcare center and its competitors each have distinct (and at times overlapping) target areas. By maximizing impressions going to target ZIP codes, the agency could save that budget and reallocate it to drive higher frequency in highly competitive areas.

Find Your Customer with Geotargeting

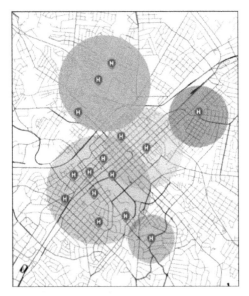

CROSS SCREEN
MEDIA

Results

With a precise media plan targeted by channel at the hyper-local level, the provider increased on-target reach by **12%**

without increasing spend. Cross Screen Media drove the improvement by 1) efficiently targeting the desired audience on the channels where they consumed media most and 2) reallocating the budget to highly competitive areas instead of spending on ads outside the target geography.

TURNING MEASUREMENT INTO INCREMENTAL REACH

Challenge

A major auto brand in the Dallas market and its agency needed to address 2 critical challenges:

- How do we accurately measure the broadcast campaign's on-target reach and frequency?
- How do we use that measurement data to drive incremental reach by adding cable and streaming TV?

The agency turned to Cross Screen Media to address both questions.

Solution

To determine the campaign's reach, we analyzed the initial broadcast ad spend for the auto brand over the

▶ **QUICK DEFINITION**

Auto Intender:
Someone in the market
to purchase a car
. . . .

course of **2** weeks in June. We looked at **3** audience segments: **18+**, adults **25–54**, and "auto intenders."

The campaign delivered **8.3M** impressions to adults **18+**, with **4.4M** going to the **25–54** group and **5M** to the auto intender group. When we deduplicated these numbers, we found that the brand's message reached about **690K** of the auto intender group or about **48%** of the total.

Auto Case Study: Who Have We Reached So Far?

	Auto Brand A	Auto Brand B
Impressions: 18+	8.3M	3.9M
Impressions: Ages 25–54	4.4M	2.0M
Impressions: Auto Intender	5.0M	2.3M
Reached: Auto Intender	690K (48%)	592K (41%)
Frequency: Auto Intender	7.2	3.5
Unreached: Auto Intender	738K (52%)	837K (59%)

CROSS SCREEN MEDIA

Just as importantly, by measuring the frequency, we saw that most of the audience was either under- or over-exposed to the campaign—only a small percentage saw the ad the number of times that the brand intended.

To identify the unreached audience, we combined the auto-intender audience with people who rarely or never watch broadcast TV. It was critical to factor in audience consumption habits, or the advertiser would have missed an entire segment of its target consumer.

Auto Case Study: Who Have We Reached So Far? *(continued)*

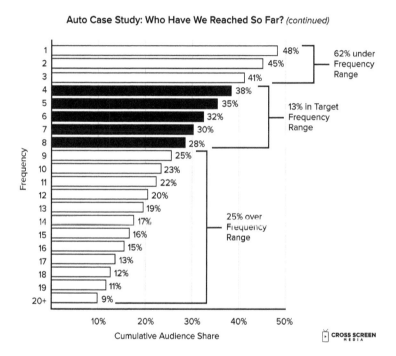

We analyzed over **58K** potential cable TV spots that could potentially reach this new audience. We applied an index to each spot to understand where the highest frequency of our target audience watched cable. For example, the highest-indexed spot was ESPNU during primetime. This option is highly efficient, as it is less expensive than other options, but it reaches the same people.

We then looked at CTV/streaming TV and digital video across mobile, desktop, and social media platforms, and we found that we could reach **35%** of that new audience through streaming TV and **66%** through digital video.

Auto Case Study: How Do They Consume Content? *(continued)*
CTV : Digital Video (including CTV)

Screen	Heavy	Light	Heavy + Light
CTV	19%	16%	**35%**
Digital Video	27%	39%	**66%**

CROSS SCREEN MEDIA

Results

Finally, we had to determine how much reach would improve with increased spending on cable and CTV. To analyze that, we took the budget for the auto brand and examined **3** different scenarios, in which we increased the advertising spend by **10%**, **20%**, and **30%**. How much incremental reach would each deliver?

Auto Case Study: What Are Our Options for Growing Reach?

Additional Budget	Cable	CTV/Digital
$17K (+10%)	+10%	+12%
$34K (+20%)	+16%	+20%
$51K (+30%)	+20%	+26%

CROSS SCREEN MEDIA

By adding **10%** to the budget, we could reach an additional **10%** through cable and an additional **12%** through streaming. Those percentages went up as the ad spend increased. The auto brand was able to take a data-driven approach to significantly increase on-target reach without having to dramatically increase its total video ad spend. Additionally, this learning informed future campaigns, creating a constant optimization cycle.

> ► **WHY THIS MATTERS**
>
> Local advertisers can find incremental reach for a lower cost by shifting dollars to underfunded channels such as streaming TV and cable.

CASE STUDY 3
GOING DEEPER ON CABLE
How a Political Agency Optimized Performance during a Pivotal Election

Challenge

A large ad agency was targeting a specific voting audience across multiple Georgia markets at the local level and needed a data-driven approach to significantly increase the impact and efficiency of its campaign. The agency had been allocating its cable ad budget (**25%** of the total) to running spots on Fox News, with the rest (**75%**) going to local broadcast.

Cable news generates a partisan audience, and political campaigns know they are reaching their base when they advertise there. The problem is that this audience continues to shrink at the same rate as linear TV overall, meaning campaigns must broaden their buy beyond nown. The agency turned to Cross Screen Media to maximize on-target reach through a more efficient allocation across channels.

Solution

Cross Screen Media quickly identified that the original TV plan would reach just **34%** of the intended target audience in the target markets, missing nearly ⅔ of desired voters.

Running an optimized TV plan that identified undervalued networks and dayparts showed that buying deeper into cable would significantly improve on-target reach without requiring additional budget.

Results

Through a deeper cable buy that added **6** more networks, the new optimized TV plan delivered **29%** incremental reach (**34%** → **44%**)—with no additional spending.

The graphics below highlight the significant increase in reach driven by the optimized plan compared to the original.

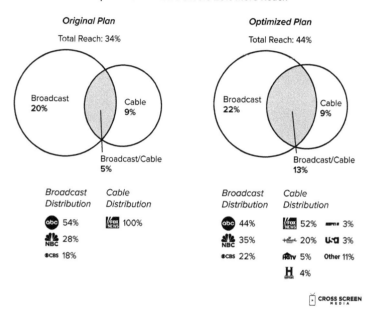

Optimized TV Plan Delivers 29% More Reach

Original Plan

Total Reach: 34%

Broadcast 20%

Cable 9%

Broadcast/Cable 5%

Broadcast Distribution
- abc 54%
- NBC 28%
- CBS 18%

Cable Distribution
- FOX NEWS 100%

Optimized Plan

Total Reach: 44%

Broadcast 22%

Cable 9%

Broadcast/Cable 13%

Broadcast Distribution
- abc 44%
- NBC 35%
- CBS 22%

Cable Distribution
- FOX NEWS 52%
- 20%
- HGTV 5%
- H 4%
- 3%
- USA 3%
- Other 11%

CROSS SCREEN MEDIA

► WHY THIS MATTERS

Most advertisers we work with find incremental reach to their target audience at a lower cost when they buy deeper on cable.

EIGHTEEN

55B REASONS LOCAL VIDEO ADVERTISING MATTERS

When it comes to local video advertising, the goals are simple: ad agencies want to reach as much of their target market as possible in the most cost-efficient way. But as people's behavior fragments and shifts away from traditional linear and cable TV and toward digital video and streaming TV, achieving these simple goals gets more complicated.

The fact is that many agencies aren't comfortable with or properly equipped to handle today's cross-screen challenges and optimize their spend to deliver optimal results.

Fortunately, there's a solution. By combining data and new local planning and measurement tools (like Cross

Screen Media), agencies can successfully navigate the **$55B** local TV and video ad market. Now it's possible to achieve our goals using methods that didn't even exist just a few years ago.

EVERYONE'S GOT THE SAME LOCAL CHALLENGES

At Cross Screen Media, we talk to many local advertisers and agencies, all experiencing the same challenges. They ask essentially the same questions:

- How much of my target market can I reach through broadcast, cable, streaming, and digital video?
- Which networks and channels are the most cost-effective?
- Is there anything I can do to reach those audiences my current buy does not reach?

The Local Ad Market Is Huge

The first thing to note is the local video market (including linear TV and streaming) is big—and getting bigger. Video accounts for **46%** of the US ad market, and local video represents **17%**. Moreover, the US video ad market is growing at 7% CAGR. This means there's a dynamic market with lots of new advertisers, new sellers, and, most importantly, new opportunities. But it will take new tools and methodologies to seize those opportunities.

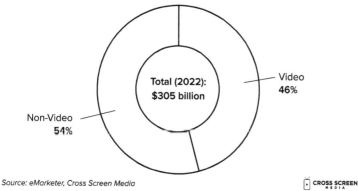

Video Accounts for 46% of the Entire US Advertising Market

Total (2022): $305 billion

Video 46%

Non-Video 54%

Source: eMarketer, Cross Screen Media

CROSS SCREEN MEDIA

Attention Continues to Shift and Fragment

People's attention continues to quickly shift away from traditional broadcast and cable and toward streaming. According to Nielsen, streaming surpassed cable for the **first** time in 2022.[80]

The streaming market poses huge challenges for agencies, however, as there are **hundreds** of channels, platforms, and devices to target. At Cross Screen Media, we

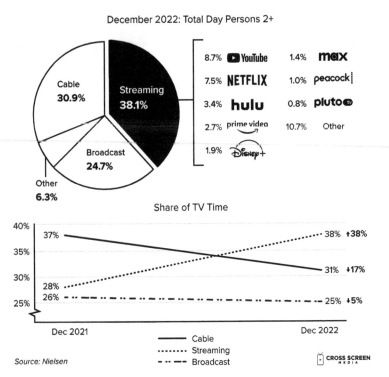

Streaming Share of Total TV Time +101% since Start of Pandemic

December 2022: Total Day Persons 2+

8.7% ▶ YouTube	1.4% max
7.5% NETFLIX	1.0% peacock
3.4% hulu	0.8% pluto⊕
2.7% prime video	10.7% Other
1.9% Disney+	

Cable 30.9%

Streaming 38.1%

Broadcast 24.7%

Other 6.3%

Share of TV Time

Dec 2021 — Dec 2022

Cable: 37% → 31% ↓17%
Streaming: 28% → 38% ↑38%
Broadcast: 26% → 25% ↓5%

Cable
Streaming
Broadcast

Source: Nielsen

CROSS SCREEN MEDIA

work with advertisers across the video-ad ecosystem, a subset of which is represented in the logos on the following page.

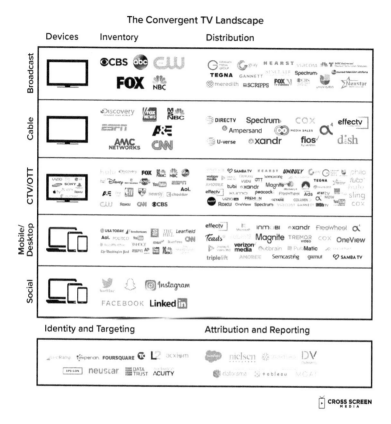

The Convergent TV Landscape

THE LOCAL AD MARKET IS COMPETITIVE

Adding to the complexity of local video is the ad-buying market itself. Unlike national advertising, where just **250** brands buy **90%** of national broadcast TV, in the local market, there are over **1M** video advertisers. This increased competition has led to higher CPMs at the local level on platforms like YouTube and Facebook.

How Many Local Video Ad Buyers Are There in the US?

		Advertising Spend (US$)	Number of Advertisers	Spend per Advertiser
National	Linear TV	$42B	250	$170M
	CTV/Mobile/Desktop	$20B	1,250	$20M
Local	Linear TV	$24B	214K	$111K
	CTV/Mobile/Desktop	$21B	951K	$11K

Source: Borrell and Associates, GroupM, eMarketer, Cross Screen Media

CROSS SCREEN MEDIA

▶ KEY BATTLE IN THE SCREEN WARS

The local video ad market will be the next battleground for convergent TV, but winning this space will require an offering built specifically for local advertisers. The same ad stack built for national advertisers with an annual video ad spend of **$50M** or more will not work for local advertisers spending an average of **$43K**.

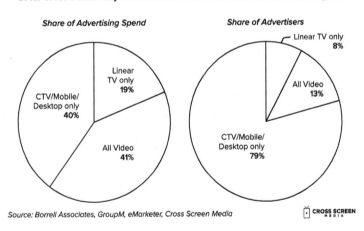

Local Cross Screen Buyers Account for 13% of Advertisers and 41% of Spend

Share of Advertising Spend

CTV/Mobile/Desktop only 40%
Linear TV only 19%
All Video 41%

Share of Advertisers

Linear TV only 8%
All Video 13%
CTV/Mobile/Desktop only 79%

Source: Borrell Associates, GroupM, eMarketer, Cross Screen Media

CROSS SCREEN MEDIA

THE FIRST KEY TO SUCCESS: BETTER PLANNING

The **first** key to better local video campaigns is better planning. Agencies can no longer afford to simply allot a percentage of their spend to "streaming" and call it a day. Using new planning tools, like Cross Screen Media, it's possible to aggregate data about your target audience and finally answer those important questions: "How much of my target market am I able to reach?" and "Which networks and channels are the most cost-effective?" Just because planning has gotten more complex, that doesn't mean it has to be hard or time-consuming.[81]

THE SECOND KEY TO SUCCESS: MEASUREMENT

The **second** key to local video success is measurement and optimization. Digital video has long offered tools for campaign measurement, and those tools are now available for linear TV sources as well, allowing agencies to see, for the first time, a complete picture of how their campaigns are performing.

▶ **WHY THIS MATTERS**

While the local video ad market is larger than many expect, it is fragmented and complex. Solutions designed for national advertisers (Super Bowl, upfronts, etc.) won't work for local advertisers.

With so many inventory options, local advertisers will benefit from starting with a clear view into reach and frequency across their channels for their precise audience.

▶ **QUICK DEFINITION**

Upfronts: An annual event where the networks showcase their planned programming for the upcoming season; advertisers can purchase advertising "up front" at a negotiated price versus later in the scatter market, which can cost **15–40%** more

. . . .

NINETEEN

CROSS-SCREEN TECH = HUGE ADVANTAGE FOR STREAMING TV

All video will move to streaming. The exact timeline is debatable, but the tectonic shift continues to accelerate as you read this. With this shift, it has become clear that the winners of the advertising world will be those who embrace the opportunity of streaming TV and invest in technology that empowers them to excel. So in the battle for streaming dominance, where does the advantage lie between buyers specializing in linear buying and planning vs. digital-**first** buyers?

Cross Screen Technology = Huge Advantage for Streaming TV

	Cross Screen Planning, Activation, and Measurement		
	TV Buyer	Digital Buyer	Who Wins Streaming?
Scenario #1	✕	✕	Digital Buyer
Scenario #2	✕	✓	Digital Buyer
Scenario #3	✓	✕	TV Buyer
Scenario #4	✓	✓	Jump Ball

CROSS SCREEN MEDIA

On the **one** hand, linear advertisers would seem to have the edge. After all, streaming TV is similar to linear TV in that it

- is viewed primarily on the big screen
- is highly viewable
- uses ads that are primarily paired with premium, longer-form content

All these components align with the benefits of linear TV, and streaming (on paper, at least) is the natural transition for cable and broadcast advertisers.

On the other hand, streaming TV is a natural fit for digital advertisers, as it

- enables granular targeting to precise audience segments
- is delivered via the internet and doesn't require more arduous broadcast/cable delivery
- uses digital metrics like CPM, as opposed to GRP/TRP from the linear TV world

▶ **QUICK DEFINITION**

Targeted Rating Points (TRP): The "target audience" exposure to advertising messages; 1 TRP is equivalent to the number of views where, on average, 1% of the target audience has seen an ad 1 time

The reality is that regardless of where advertisers are coming from, the demand for driving incremental, viewable, and targeted reach is growing. Streaming TV advertising is the perfect medium with which to pursue this goal, and the most successful advertisers will incorporate streaming as a central part of a holistic media plan that includes linear TV and other forms of digital video.

To create the optimal media plan by market and for each specific audience segment, this new breed of cross-screen advertisers will need to use a common set of metrics to make apples-to-apples comparisons across all screens.

▶ **WHY THIS MATTERS**

In the future, there will not be linear TV or streaming TV buyers. There will only be convergent TV buyers.

Brands and agencies are investing in specialized cross-screen planning and measurement technology solutions that do the heavy lifting of incorporating data and making clear comparisons across rates, consumption habits, and audience targeting. The cross-screen consumer is already here, and siloed planning and buying won't cut it anymore. Advertisers need to become cross-screen, too, or audiences will leave them behind.

▶ **WHY THIS MATTERS**

Whoever controls the streaming TV ad budget controls the overall video ad budget. Streaming is ground zero for video advertisers.

· ·

TWENTY

CONCLUSION

It has been **15** years since Netflix launched streaming and forever changed what we think of as TV. The next major change will be in advertising. Over the next decade, TV advertising will shift from predominantly linear to streaming.

This shift will happen in the following **4** steps:

1. **2025:** Streaming TV surpasses linear TV in total reach
2. **2026:** Streaming TV surpasses linear TV in time spent
3. **2028:** Streaming TV surpasses linear TV in ad spend

4. **2030**: Streaming TV surpasses linear TV in ad impressions

As I have written in this book, there will be winners and losers. Some huge networks today will go out of business while others will merge (à la Warner Bros. and Discovery). New arrivals will emerge and out-innovate the competition, accounting for a major slice of our media diet, like what Netflix has done over the past **15** years. The winners that remain will fight over a larger market, which I describe through our "Rule of **100**" framework:

1. **100%** of TV will be streamed
2. **100%** of TV advertising will be streamed
3. **100X** advertiser base vs. national TV today
4. **$100** CPMs
5. **$100B** TV ad market in the US

The TV advertising base will be driven by demand from **100X** more advertisers than exist today, driving CPMs higher than most anticipate, benefiting networks. Viewed through today's TV ad market lens, **$100** CPMs would seem like a terrible deal for advertisers. I disagree. Advertisers will utilize better targeting and measurement, allowing them to focus a greater share of their TV advertising dollars on the right targets and content. This will lead to lower eCPMs for advertisers and a win-win for the industry.

For advertisers, the growth of streaming and other digital platforms has created vast opportunities to use video to get messages out. Never have you had so many options for delivering ads to precisely the audience you want to reach. In the old days of linear TV, it wasn't hard to find viewers; they were clustered around their sets watching *M*A*S*H* and *60 Minutes*. Today, they're scattered across the vast and ever-expanding media landscape. Advertisers who "crack the code" of this new paradigm are rewarded with robust data they can use to expand their audience and create even more effective video ads.

If your target customer never sees your ad, nothing else you do matters. It won't matter how good your ad is or how often you run it. Fragmented customer attention is already a headache for advertisers, and it will only get more complicated as viewers migrate from linear TV to streaming TV and the number of shows and streaming providers continues to expand.

Successful advertisers will put the customer at the center of their plans. Your TV ads should be running where your customers are watching today, rather than where they were watching 15 years ago. Take full advantage of streaming TV's ability to offer targeting and measurement.

In a past life, I was in your shoes. I built Cross Screen Media to give local advertisers like you the tools needed to succeed in the convergent TV world.

▶ BOTTOM LINE

I am here to help. Drop me a line, and let's win the battle for attention with convergent TV. Together, we can do this!

. . . .

Michael Beach

CEO, Cross Screen Media

mbeach@crossscreen.media

HOW TO WORK WITH MICHAEL

1. I want to explore more resources about the book:
   ScreenWarsBook.com
2. I want to learn more about the author:
   MichaelBeach.com
3. I want to become a convergent TV advertiser:
   CrossScreenMedia.com
4. I have a data or media company that I want to sell:
   1903Group.com
5. I have an early-stage data or media startup looking
   for investors: *ScreenWarsFund.com*
6. I am a reporter looking to speak with Michael:
   MichaelBeach.com/Press
7. I would like Michael to speak to my company:
   ScreenWarsMedia.com

CROSS SCREEN MEDIA RESOURCES

1. **1.2K+** blog posts, case studies, white papers, webinars, and more: *CrossScreenMedia.com*
2. Weekly newsletter focused on convergent TV advertising: *StateOfTheScreens.com*
3. **50+** podcasts: *ScreenWarsPod.com*

TABLES AND CHARTS

A downloadable PDF of all the tables and charts in this book is available at *ScreenWarsBook.com*.

GLOSSARY OF TERMS

Addressable Advertising: The targeting of a specific audience (auto intenders, swing voters, etc.) on a **1:1** basis, at either the household or the individual level

Ad Frequency: The average number of times households or individuals view an advertisement during a specific time period

Ad Impressions: The individual occurrences of advertising content being displayed, whether or not it is viewed

Ad Reach: The total number of different individuals or households exposed, at least once, to an advertisement during a given period; **Reach Percentage:** The percentage of individuals or households exposed, calculated as (# of Individuals Reached) ÷ (# of Individuals in the Total Audience)

Ad Viewability: An advertising metric that quantifies how much of an ad is actually seen; for video ads, there is a range of industry standards with minimums as low as 2 seconds (at Cross Screen Media, we use a minimum of 5 seconds before we consider an ad watched)

Affiliate Fees/Revenue (aka "Carriage Fees"): The fees paid to networks (ESPN, etc.) by pay-TV providers (Comcast, etc.) for the right to carry a channel

Auto Intender: Someone in the market to purchase a car

Behavioral Data/Targeting: The targeting of a group of people or an audience, based on their affinity or likeness to perform a particular behavior (purchase a sedan, apply for an insurance quote, etc.); behavioral targeting is more accurate than untargeted advertising but less accurate than first-party targeting methods

Broadcast TV: Television that is delivered over the air via terrestrial antenna systems

Cable TV: Television that is delivered locally via coaxial cable or fiber-optic transmission

Churn: A subscriber canceling their subscription

Compound Annual Growth Rate (CAGR): Average annual growth rate over a period of time (years, etc.)

Connected TV (CTV): Any television connected directly to the internet for video streaming; used interchangeably with "Streaming TV" throughout this book

Convergent TV: Linear TV + Streaming TV

Convergent TV Advertising: Linear TV advertising + Streaming TV advertising

Cost Per Mille (CPM): The cost per 1K ad impressions, an industry-standard measure for selling ads, calculated as (Total Cost ÷ Impressions) × 1,000

Demand-Side Platform (DSP): A system in which advertisers buying digital advertising inventory can activate and manage campaigns across hundreds of publishers aggregated into a single interface; DSPs also allow advertisers to adjust campaigns midflight instead of having to wait until the campaign has concluded

Digital Video Advertising: Any ad delivered on a digital device, including mobile phones, tablets, desktop computers, and connected televisions (CTV)

Effective CPM (eCPM): The effective cost per 1K impressions, calculated as CPM ÷ (Viewability %) ÷ (On-Target %); for digital ads, this means on-target, viewable, 5-second views

Gross Rating Points (GRP): The "total audience" exposure to advertising messages; 1 GRP is equivalent to the number of views where, on average, 1% of the total (not target) audience has seen an ad 1 time

Linear TV: The traditional television system in which a viewer watches a scheduled TV program when it's broadcasted and on its original channel

Measurement: Finding out the actual reach, frequency, and outcomes of an advertising campaign; cross-screen measurement is increasingly critical as advertisers place ads across linear TV, CTV, and digital video

Media Buying (aka "Activation"): A method that marketing agencies apply after a media planner completes their research and builds a campaign strategy; media buyers use this strategy to find and bid on ad inventory across multiple ad channels

Pay-TV: A bundle of TV networks, such as a cable TV package, purchased as a subscription

Streaming TV: An online service that allows subscribers to watch TV shows and movies over the internet (Netflix, Hulu, etc.); used interchangeably with "Connected TV (CTV)" throughout this book

Targeted Rating Points (TRP): The "target audience" exposure to advertising messages; 1 TRP is equivalent to the number of views where, on average, **1%** of the target audience has seen an ad **1** time

TVOS: TV operating system

Upfronts: An annual event where the networks showcase their planned programming for the upcoming season; advertisers can purchase advertising "up front" at a negotiated price versus later in the scatter market, which can cost **15–40%** more

NOTES

1   US Bureau of Labor Statistics, "American Time Use Survey—2021 Results," news release no. USDL-22-1261, June 23, 2022, https://www.bls.gov/news.release/archives/atus_06232022.htm.

2   Jason Yang, "How Many TVs Are In Your Home? More Than You Think!" *Apartment Therapy*, Dec. 19, 2019, https://www.apartmenttherapy.com/how-many-tvs-is-too-many-tvs-158173.

3   Nielsen, "More than Half the Homes in U.S. Have Three or More TVs," July 2009, https://www.nielsen.com/insights/2009/more-than-half-the-homes-in-us-have-three-or-more-tvs/.

4   Rachel Krantz-Kent, "Television, Capturing America's Attention at Prime Time and Beyond," *Beyond the Numbers* 7, no. 14 (Sept. 2018), https://www.bls.gov/opub/btn/volume-7/television-capturing-americas-attention.htm.

5   eMarketer, "Average Time Spent per Day with TV, US, 2021–2025," accessed Feb. 6, 2024, https://forecasts-na1.emarketer.com/584b26021403070290f93a3b/5851918b0626310a2c186b45.

6   Jessica Lis, "US Time Spent with Connected Devices 2022: A Return to Pre-Pandemic Growth," *Insider Intelligence*, June 9, 2022, https://content-na1.emarketer.com/us-time-spent-with-connected-devices-2022.

7   US Bureau of Labor Statistics, "American Time Use Survey," https://www.bls.gov/news.release/archives/atus_06232022.htm.

8   Leichtman Research Group, "Major Pay-TV Providers Lost about 5,900,000 Subscribers in 2022," news release, March 3, 2023,

https://www.leichtmanresearch.com/major-pay-tv-providers-lost-about-5900000-subscribers-in-2022/.

9   "Data: 87% of US Homes Have SVoD Service," Advanced Television, March 29, 2023, https://advanced-television. com/2023/03/29/data-87-of-us-homes-have-svod-service/.

10   Robert Williams, "Streaming Households Don't Always Cancel Pay TV," *Research Intelligencer*, MediaPost, Jan. 12, 2023, https://www.mediapost.com/publications/article/381515/streaming-households-dont-always-cancel-pay-tv.html.

11   Lyndon Seitz, "14 Fascinating Cord Cutting Statistics In 2024," Broadband Search, Jan. 4, 2024, https://www.broadbandsearch. net/blog/cord-cutting-statistics.

12   Nielsen, "Streaming Services Remain Most Popular Destination for TV Viewing in December," Jan. 2023, https://www.nielsen. com/insights/2023/streaming-services-remain-most-popular-destination-for-tv-viewing-in-december/.

13   eMarketer, "Connected TV Households, US, 2023–2027," accessed Feb. 6, 2024, https://forecasts-na1.emarketer.com/ 584b26021403070290f93a3a/5851918a0626310a2c1869b5?_gl=1* 13g5erg*_ga*MTQ2ODE1OTA5LjE2ODIyOTg3NTI.*_ga_XXYLHB 9SXG*MTY4NDI3NDk3NC44LjEuMTY4NDI3NTA3OS4wLjAuMA. &_ga=2.127273613.1066059568.1684275080-146815909. 1682298752.

14   "Super Bowl Ratings History (1967–present)," Sports Media Watch, accessed Jan. 30, 2024, https://www.sportsmediawatch.com/super-bowl-ratings-historical-viewership-chart-cbs-nbc-fox-abc/.

15   Wilson Chapman, "John Landgraf Says Cost-Cutting Is Good for White Men, Not for Diversity," *IndieWire*, Jan. 12, 2023, https://www.indiewire.com/features/general/peak-tv-2022-john-landgraf-diversity-1234799297/.

16   "Where Can TV Grow Amid Declining National Ad Sales?," *Radio and Television Business Report*, Aug. 10, 2017, https://www.rbr. com/where-can-tv-grow-amid-declining-national-ad-sales/.

17   "Wayne Gretzky > Quotes > Quotable Quote," Goodreads, accessed Jan. 30, 2024, https://www.goodreads.com/ quotes/8609851-i-skate-to-where-the-puck-is-going-to-be.

18 Wikipedia, s.v. "History of Television," last modified Jan. 29, 2024, 9:07, https://en.wikipedia.org/wiki/History_of_television.

19 Elon University, "1920s–1960s: Television," *Imagining the Internet: A History and Forecast*, accessed Jan. 30, 2024, https://www.elon.edu/u/imagining/time-capsule/150-years/back-1920-1960.

20 Wikipedia, s.v. "Top-Rated United States Television Programs by Season," last modified Sept. 26, 2023, 1:06, https://en.wikipedia.org/wiki/Top-rated_United_States_television_programs_by_season.

21 Brian Lowry, "'M*A*S*H' Said Goodbye 40 Years Ago, with a Finale for the Ages," *CNN*, Feb. 28, 2023, https://www.cnn.com/2023/02/28/entertainment/mash-finale/index.html.

22 Sara Fischer, "Axios Media Trends," *Axios*, May 21, 2019, https://www.axios.com/newsletters/axios-media-trends-1245102a-65f3-4dc4-8b50-2b7e6cfc5d30.html.

23 "93 Million Toast End of 'Cheers,'" *Los Angeles Times*, May 22, 1993, https://www.latimes.com/archives/la-xpm-1993-05-22-ca-38413-story.html.

24 Victor Garrett, "The 11 Most-Watched HBO Series to Date, Ranked," *MovieWeb*, Jan. 10, 2023, https://movieweb.com/most-watched-hbo-series/.

25 Encyclopedia.com, s.v. "Cable Television, History of," accessed Jan. 31, 2024, https://www.encyclopedia.com/media/encyclopedias-almanacs-transcripts-and-maps/cable-television-history.

26 George Mannes, "The Birth of Cable TV," *Invention & Technology* 12, no. 2 (Fall 1996), https://www.inventionandtech.com/content/birth-cable-tv-1.

27 NCTA, "History of Cable Television," archived March 1, 2013, at the Wayback Machine, https://web.archive.org/web/20100905133543/http://www.ncta.com/About/About/HistoryofCableTelevision.aspx.

28 Colin Keeley, "John Malone Operating Manual (Cable Cowboy Book Summary & Takeaways)," blog post, accessed Jan. 31, 2024, https://www.colinkeeley.com/blog/john-malone-operating-manual-cable-cowboy-book-summary.

29 Television History—The First 75 Years, "Television Facts and Statistics—1939 to 2000," archived Aug. 19, 2022, at the Wayback

Machine, https://web.archive.org/web/20220819180459/https://
www.tvhistory.tv/facts-stats.htm.

30 Daniel Frankel, "With DirecTV Now Shrinking at Nearly 17%,
MoffettNathanson Says Pay TV Has Entered the 'Doom Cycle,'"
NextTV, May 14, 2023, https://www.nexttv.com/news/with-directv-
now-shrinking-at-nearly-17-moffettnathanson-says-pay-tv-has-
entered-the-doom-cycle.

31 Sam Ro, "Americans Are Paying for a Lot of Channels They
Don't Watch," *Business Insider*, Oct. 25, 2015, https://www.
businessinsider.com/number-of-cable-channels-received-vs-
viewed-2015-10.

32 Joe Mandese, "Exclusive Nielsen Data Reveals Number of
TV Channels Received Plummeting," *Research Intelligencer*,
MediaPost, Feb. 13, 2020, https://www.mediapost.com/
publications/article/347037/exclusive-nielsen-data-reveals-
number-of-tv-channe.html.

33 jaimenish, "The History of Cable Television," Timetoast, accessed
Jan. 31, 2024, https://www.timetoast.com/timelines/31741.

34 Kelsey Sutton, "Covid-19's Economic Fallout Will Accelerate
Linear TV's Collapse," *Adweek*, June 11, 2020, https://www.
adweek.com/convergent-tv/covid-19s-economic-fallout-will-
accelerate-linear-tvs-collapse/.

35 Nathan McAlone, "Cable TV Price Increases Have Beaten
Inflation Every Single Year for 20 Years," *Business Insider*, Oct. 31,
2016, https://www.businessinsider.com/cable-tv-prices-inflation-
chart-2016-10.

36 Scott Robson, "Economics of Basic Cable Networks 2022,"
Market Intelligence, S&P Global, Nov. 28, 2022, https://www.
capitaliq.spglobal.com/web/client?auth=inherit#news/
article?id=72770307.

37 Michael Schneider, "Most-Watched Television Networks:
Ranking 2022's Winners and Losers," *Variety*, Dec. 29, 2022,
https://variety.com/2022/tv/news/most-watched-channels-2022-
tv-network-ratings-1235475170/.

38 Ian Morris, "Netflix Is Now Bigger than Cable TV," *Forbes*, June
13, 2017, https://www.forbes.com/sites/ianmorris/2017/06/13/
netflix-is-now-bigger-than-cable-tv/?sh=52208d8f158b.

39 Seth Fiegerman, "How Netflix Beat Its Rivals and Survived the 2000s," *CNN*, July 24, 2018, https://money.cnn.com/2018/07/24/technology/netflix-2000s/index.html.

40 Patrick Kariuki, "How and When Did Netflix Start? A Brief History of the Company," *MUO*, Feb. 14, 2023, https://www.makeuseof.com/how-when-netflix-start-brief-company-history.

41 Product Habits, "How Netflix Became a $100 Billion Company in 20 Years," blog post, accessed Jan. 31, 2024, https://producthabits.com/how-netflix-became-a-100-billion-company-in-20-years/.

42 Edward F. O'Keefe, "Streaming War Won," Harvard Kennedy School Shorenstein Center on Media, Politics and Public Policy, April 29, 2019, https://shorensteincenter.org/streaming-war-won/.

43 Tim Arango, "Time Warner Views Netflix as a Fading Star," The New York Times, Dec. 12, 2010, https://www.nytimes.com/2010/12/13/business/media/13bewkes.html.

44 John Fletcher, "The History of US Broadband," *Market Intelligence*, S&P Global, May 9, 2023, https://www.capitaliq.spglobal.com/web/client?auth=inherit#news/article?id=75534068&KeyProductLinkType=58&utm_source=MIAlerts&utm_medium=realtime-minewsresearch-newsfeature-sector%20spotlight&utm_campaign=Alert_Email&redirected=1.

45 Peter Kafka, "How HBO Could Have Become—or Bought—Netflix," *Vox*, Nov. 18, 2021, https://www.vox.com/recode/22788096/hbo-netflix-apple-book-tindberbox-james-andrew-miller.

46 Tara Bitran, "Skip Intro: Netflix Turns 25 Today," *Tudum* by Netflix, Aug. 29, 2022, https://www.netflix.com/tudum/articles/netflix-trivia-25th-anniversary.

47 Dan Burrows, "If You'd Put $1,000 into Netflix Stock 20 Years Ago, Here's What You'd Have Today," *Kiplinger*, Nov. 8, 2023, https://www.kiplinger.com/invested-1000-in-netflix-nflx-stock-worth-how-much-now.

48 Todd Spangler, "Apple CEO: 'We Don't Make Purely Financial Decisions' about Apple TV Plus Content," *Variety*, Jan. 27, 2022, https://variety.com/2022/digital/news/apple-tv-plus-purely-financial-decisions-ceo-tim-cook-1235165656/.

49 Michael Beach, "The Streaming Decade in Four Steps," *State of the Screens* (blog), Cross Screen Media, June 8, 2023, https://crossscreen.media/state-of-the-screens/the-streaming-decade-in-four-steps/.

50 Leichtman Research Group, "49% of Adults Watch Video via a Connected TV Device Daily," news release, June 2, 2023, https://leichtmanresearch.com/49-of-adults-watch-video-via-a-connected-tv-device-daily/.

51 Kevin Tran, "Top Media & Tech Companies to Spend $140 Billion on Content in 2022," *Variety*, Jan. 11, 2022, https://variety.com/vip/top-media-tech-companies-to-spend-140-billion-on-content-in-2022-1235150688/.

52 Amanda Cataldo and Daniela Gama, "The 15 Most Expensive TV Series Ever Made, Ranked," *Collider*, Jan. 10, 2024, https://collider.com/most-expensive-tv-series-ever-made/.

53 Jonathan Carson, "Antenna Q3 2022 SVOD Growth Report: As the World Churns," Antenna, accessed Jan. 31, 2024, https://www.antenna.live/post/antenna-q3-2022-svod-growth-report-as-the-world-churns.

54 Doug Shapiro, "To Everything, Churn, Churn, Churn: How Churn Became Streaming TV's Biggest Surprise and Biggest Problem," Medium, Nov. 17, 2022, https://dougshapiro.medium.com/to-everything-churn-churn-churn-b9044d376be.

55 Benjamin Mullin and David Marcelis, "Disney+, HBO Max and Other Streamers Get Waves of Subscribers from Must-See Content. Keeping Them Is Hard.," *The Wall Street Journal*, Jan. 31, 2022, https://www.wsj.com/articles/streaming-data-netflix-hbo-disney-hulu-11643560207.

56 Adam Chitwood, "'Ozark' Showrunner Explains Why Season 4 Was Split in 2 Parts," *TheWrap*, Jan. 13, 2022, https://www.thewrap.com/why-ozark-season-4-split-in-two-parts/.

57 Ashley Rodriguez, "Roku Insiders Detail How It Beat Out Amazon and Google to Dominate Streaming TV and Expand Its Ad Business, but Created New Challenges and Rankled Some Partners," *Business Insider*, Dec. 22, 2020, https://www.businessinsider.com/inside-rokus-ad-growth-battle-for-platform-dominance-with-amazon-2020-12.

58   Gavin Bridge, "Fading Ratings: A Special Report on TV's Shrinking Audiences," *Variety*, Jan. 4, 2022, https://variety.com/vip-special-reports/fading-ratings-a-special-report-on-tvs-shrinking-audiences-1235142986/.

59   David Bauder, "CBS Retools Streaming Service to Better Resemble TV Network," Associated Press, Jan. 24, 2022, https://apnews.com/article/technology-entertainment-business-television-arts-and-entertainment-7644e99822cc572ff692780eeaa90f47.

60   Wikipedia, s.v. "CNN," last modified Feb. 1, 2024, 1:53, https://en.wikipedia.org/wiki/CNN.

61   Sara Fischer, "Scoop: The Numbers behind CNN+," *Axios*, April 26, 2022, https://www.axios.com/2022/04/26/cnn-plus-pitch-deck-subscribers.

62   Pew Research Center, "Social Media and News Fact Sheet," Nov. 15, 2023, https://www.pewresearch.org/journalism/fact-sheet/social-media-and-news-fact-sheet/.

63   Vizio, "Vizio Holding Corp. Reports Q4 and Full Year 2021 Financial Results," news release, March 3, 2022, https://s29.q4cdn.com/107810760/files/doc_financials/2021/q1/ER-2-Q4'21-Earnings-Press-Release.pdf.

64   Statista, "Smart TV Users in the United States, 2016–2022," accessed Oct. 5, 2022, https://www.statista.com/statistics/718737/number-of-smart-tv-users-in-the-us/.

65   Vizio, "VIZIO Launches Direct Advertising Business," news release, Dec. 10, 2019, https://platformplus.vizio.com/news/vizio-launches-direct-advertising-business.

66   Nellie Andreeva, "Peak TV: Scripted Originals Rebounded in 2021 to Hit New Record Despite Pandemic, FX Tally Reveals," *Deadline*, Jan. 14, 2022, https://deadline.com/2022/01/peak-tv-scripted-originals-2021-new-record-pandemic-fx-tally-1234913192/.

67   Kasey Moore, "Netflix Originals Now Make Up 50% of Overall US Library," *What's on Netflix*, Oct. 26, 2023, https://www.whats-on-netflix.com/news/50-of-netflixs-library-is-now-made-of-netflix-originals/.

68   Television History, "Television Facts and Statistics," https://web.archive.org/web/20220819180459/https://www.tvhistory.tv/facts-stats.htm.

69   William M. O'Barr, "The Rise and Fall of the TV Commercial,"
      Advertising & Society Review 11, no. 2 (2010), https://doi.
      org/10.1353/asr.0.0049.

70   William Harris, "What Are the Effects of DVR on Advertising?,"
      HowStuffWorks, accessed Feb. 1, 2024, https://people.
      howstuffworks.com/culture-traditions/tv-and-culture/effects-of-
      dvr-on-advertising.htm.

71   Douglas Galbi, "U.S. Advertising Expenditure Data," *purple motes*
      (blog), Sept. 14, 2008, https://www.purplemotes.net/2008/09/14/
      us-advertising-expenditure-data/.

72   Sara Lebow, "Has TV Ad Spending Hit Its Peak in the US?,"
      Insider Intelligence, Apr. 12, 2022, https://www.insiderintelligence.
      com/content/has-tv-ad-spending-hit-its-peak-us.

73   Kate Scott-Dawkins, "This Year Next Year: Global 2022 End-of-
      Year Forecast," GroupM, Dec. 5, 2022, https://www.groupm.com/
      longform/this-year-next-year-global-2022-end-of-year-forecast/.

74   "Where Can TV Grow," *Radio and Television Business Report*,
      https://www.rbr.com/where-can-tv-grow-amid-declining-national-
      ad-sales/.

75   Michael Beach, "55 Billion Reasons to Care about Local Video
      Ads," *State of the Screens* (blog), Cross Screen Media, April 20,
      2022, https://crossscreen.media/state-of-the-screens/55-billion-
      reasons-to-care-about-local-video-ads-2.

76   iSpot.tv, "2022 TV Advertising Year-in-Review," Jan. 5, 2023,
      https://www.ispot.tv/hub/resources/free-reports/2022-tv-
      advertising-year-in-review.

77   Anthony Crupi, "Unsinkable Live Sports Find Safe Harbor in
      Stormy TV Ad Market," *Sportico*, March 10, 2023, https://www.
      sportico.com/business/media/2023/broadcast-cable-sports-ad-
      sales-uncertainty-1234711995.

78   Tim Peterson, "Future of TV Briefing: How Top Streamers' Ad
      Prices Have Trended in This Year's Upfront Negotiations,"
      Digiday, Aug. 2, 2023, https://digiday.com/future-of-tv/future-of-
      tv-briefing-how-top-streamers-ad-prices-have-trended-in-this-
      years-upfront-negotiations/.

79   Dan Siroker, "Obama's $60 Million Dollar Experiment," blog
      post, Optimizely, Nov. 29, 2010, https://www.optimizely.com/

insights/blog/how-obama-raised-60-million-by-running-a-simple-experiment/.

80   Michael Beach, "Nielsen Gauge: Streaming Percentage Up, Overall Usage Down," *State of the Screens* (blog), Cross Screen Media, Sept. 23, 2022, https://xscstaging.wpengine.com/state-of-the-screens/nielsen-gauge-streaming-percentage-up-overall-usage-down/.

81   Learn more about what's possible in this article I wrote: "Why Local Planning Requires Local Tools," Cross Screen Media, Sept. 7, 2022, https://xscstaging.wpengine.com/articles/why-local-planning-requires-local-tools.

Printed in the USA
CPSIA information can be obtained
at www.ICGtesting.com
CBHW072136220524
8980CB00006B/52

9 798990 229815